# SHAMELESS

# ANDREA MCLEAN

# SHAMELESS

Finding freedom & resilience
through failure

First published in Great Britain in 2026 by
DK RED, an imprint of
Dorling Kindersley Limited
20 Vauxhall Bridge Road,
London SW1V 2SA

The authorized representative in the EEA is
Dorling Kindersley Verlag GmbH. Arnulfstr. 124,
80636 Munich, Germany

Cover design by Jordan Lambley
Cover photography by Mark Harrison
Extract from Philip Larkin, 'This Be The Verse', *The Complete Poems*, Edited
by Archie Burnett, Faber & Faber, 2012, courtesy of Faber and Faber Ltd

A CIP catalogue record for this book
is available from the British Library.
ISBN: 978-0-2417-6281-3

Printed and bound in the United Kingdom
**www.dk.com**

MIX
Paper | Supporting
responsible forestry
FSC™ C018179

This book was made with Forest
Stewardship Council™ certified
paper – one small step in DK's
commitment to a sustainable future.
**Learn more at www.dk.com/uk/
information/sustainability**

For my wingman

# CONTENTS

# PROLOGUE

Before we get started, let me ask you a question.

What's one thing you don't want me to know about you?

Take your time…

I know you're figuring out what you could say.

But don't tell me that.

Tell me the *other* thing…

That one.

The thing you haven't told a living soul because you can't bear the shame.

It's okay. We all have something. We just don't tell anyone.

Until now.

# INTRODUCTION

*"If you did something wrong, don't let anybody take your mistake and use it against you. It belongs to you. It's yours. Own it."*[1]

*Salma Hayek, Actress and Producer*

I've screwed up. *Again*. As I write this, I am weeks away from being evicted from my home, our car is about to be repossessed, and the only regular phone calls I receive are from debt collectors, who are relentless in their commitment to getting what is owed to them. My parents only know a fraction of the problems I am having as I don't want to worry them, but still they ask the question, "How do you sleep with all this going on? How are you coping?"

How am I coping? As well as the next person would in this situation, I suppose. My brain whirrs and swings from clutching at straws and trying to find possible solutions to worst-case scenarios and spiralling into despair.

The clutching at straws happens during the day and takes the form of wild ideas and feverish hours spent trying to bring them to fruition: what am I good at, and how can I make money doing it? And while I am doing this, what else can I sell to pay the bills and buy groceries? I have sold my furniture, clothes, and the small amount of jewellery I had. I have already taken out every loan possible and maxed-out my credit card and overdraft to pay for everyday necessities. I have drained savings accounts set up for the children, praying that one day soon I will be able to put the money back so I can give them what I'd always hoped I could, some money towards a car or a flat.

The spiralling into hopelessness and despair takes place at night. That's when my thoughts lose coherence and become a whirr, and my body stops being my body: it is a living, pulsating ball of stress and fear. That's why, when my mum asks me how I am sleeping, I almost tell her the truth: "Oh, you know, some nights I lie awake for hours, choking on the bile of overwhelming fear. But other nights it's not so bad." Instead, I reply, "I do yoga, and that really helps."

It is the shame that keeps me silent. Shame that makes me want to minimise just how badly things have turned out, that makes me want to put on a brave face and pretend I'm okay. It's also the shame that isolates me, preventing others from really knowing what is going on and being able to help me – or at least truly *see* me.

Shame makes us feel "seen" in an entirely different way: like a stress dream where you are naked and everyone is staring at you, and you just want to wake up and be relieved that it never actually happened. I once dreamt that I'd been asked to interview the winner of *The X Factor* live from Glastonbury Festival, in front of a crowd of hundreds of thousands, and many more millions at home. I was standing in the wings, waiting for Simon Cowell to welcome me on stage, when he announced, "Now Andrea McLean is going to sing an aria from her favourite opera *Carmen* for us!" Before I could object, I was shoved on stage to sing – and, worse, I was completely and utterly *naked*. I walked about for a bit, grinning and pretending I was absolutely fine (as you do), but inside I was dying of shame. It was hideous in every way. I don't even know the words to any songs from *Carmen*.

I woke up from that nightmare, but I'm still living through this one. I suppose, metaphorically, I am about to expose myself in a way I have never done before. And I'm scared. So why do it? Why write a book about shame while in the middle of a shameful experience? Why don't I just walk around pretending I am fine (though maybe this time not singing from *Carmen*)? Because I don't want to fear being seen anymore. I want you to truly see me. I'm hoping that when you do, shame will lose some of its power – and maybe it'll help *you* let others see you, too.

We all have something that we push down and hide away, vowing never to let it see light or breathe air in case it springs to life, invigorated by the energetic force of other people's knowing.

It may be our family circumstances, our financial situation, what's happening behind closed doors in our relationship, something from our past, or perhaps something that we are living through in our present. Either way, it has a choke hold over us. It is a very particular kind of fear, that one day we will be found out. Exposed. Shamed.

It's horrible, and it can keep us feeling so alone.

But it doesn't *have* to.

This book is for those who have made errors of judgement or have simply had life throw experiences their way that have made them feel or seem "less than" in society's view, and who are buckling under the weight of their shame. I imagine this means it's for all of us. And that's the first thing I hope you take from this book: that you are *not alone*. It's not just you – it's every single one of us. And I hope that this book will help you feel less, well, *shit* about yourself.

But this book is also for everyone who wants to challenge their experience with shame. To better understand that the things you've been feeling bad about – whether it's you as a person, your experiences, circumstances, or actions, past or present – can be

We all have
something that we
push down and hide
away, vowing never
to let it see light or
breathe air in case
it springs to life,
invigorated by the
energetic force of
other people's
knowing

reframed as an opportunity to grow in resilience and connect with others with vulnerability and authenticity.

I am not covering every single thing that we as humans feel shame about; I am sticking to those that I have experience in and can offer a personal perspective on. That's why I have chosen to discuss the shame of debt, loss of identity and status, workplace difficulties, parenting missteps, relationship failure and sex. It's a pretty meaty list to get stuck into, and I have a rich seam to tap when it comes to either screwing up or experiencing challenging things! I'll be revealing the moments that have left me with crippling shame, all in the hope that by sharing my own truths, you'll feel a little lighter about the burden you carry. I'll also draw on lessons from others who have fallen down and got back up again, and the work of psychologists, sociologists, and behavioural scientists who have made it their life's work to understand why we behave in the way we do.

They say to never ask directions from someone who hasn't been where you want to go; experience matters, so you can trust that everything I'll share with you has been through my own experience of trying, failing, and failing some more. I only have one thing to ask of you as we begin this journey together: *stay with me*. We are going to go through a lot, and there will be moments where you want to look away. Don't. Stay until the end. I promise it will be worth it, because the "me" who started writing this book is not the me who finished it, as you'll discover.

I'm taking one for the team here; you don't have to tell the world about your experiences, but I hope that reading about mine will help you to step out into the world *shamelessly*.

**1**

# PHEW, IT'S NOT JUST ME

*What Is Shame Anyway?*

*"Guilt says what I did was not good.*
*Shame says I am no good."*[2]

*John Bradshaw, Author and Speaker*

When I quit my high-profile job as the longest-serving anchor of an award-winning Daytime TV show, in the middle of the global coronavirus pandemic in 2020, I did it because I felt that if we were all going to die, I wanted to die doing something I loved.

And so, I announced to millions of people watching that I wanted to be brave, paraphrasing the famous line from a beautiful poem by Erin Hansen,[3] I said: "I need to be brave. I need to know if I will fall or if I will fly."

That makes it sound a lot cooler than it was. I actually gulped, choked, and ugly cried my way through resigning from my job on national TV. It wasn't a great look. And – spoiler alert – it turns out that I *can't* fly.

Jumping off a ledge and being momentarily airborne is not the same as flying. I realised this three years after I left, when I, figuratively and financially speaking, plummeted from a great height and landed flat on my face. It was embarrassing, horrifically shameful, and I'm going to share all the gory details with you. But let me say, although this was a horrific encounter with shame, it certainly wasn't my first. Shame is a feeling that my brain and body recognise from many years of dancing together, because shame is a universal experience, and it starts young.

I'll be delving deeper into how childhood experiences impact the way we react to life's ups and down as adults a little later in the book. But I thought it would be useful to first talk a little about how our ideas about our sense of self, and the shame that is often bound up in that, start early.

## Internalised shame

In childhood, the idea of shame emerges from around 15–24 months.[4] This is around the time when we realise that our actions cause a reaction, and we are naturally testing boundaries, so we get chastised by our caregivers. We might not remember going through this ourselves, but any parent of a toddler knows this time well. Most of us probably deserved the tellings-off that we got; acting out is part of growing up, pushing boundaries and understanding what's acceptable and what's not in your home. But for many, this disciplining will have felt shameful. Knowing what we know now about the power of words and the impact they have on young minds, it seems inconceivable to think that when we were growing up parents would routinely say, "You are a bad boy!" or "You are a bad girl!" to their children, but this change from "*You are* naughty" to "*That* was a naughty thing to do" is a recent and powerful thing.

As children, we don't understand that our caregivers are flawed, and so we think that *we* are the problem. Even if a parent's response feels unfair, as a child we will still rationalise that we must somehow be at fault, because they are the adults and they are in charge. This can lead to internalised shame, where we tell ourselves, "I am not lovable", or "If I don't do this perfectly, I will be rejected."

We will have felt bad for doing what we did because it was pointed out that we had caused someone pain, or been disrespectful, or whatever. This momentary shame is normally enough to remind us not to do that thing again; we don't like how it feels so we try to avoid it. But sometimes we internalise the shame and believe that there is something wrong or unlovable about us at our core. That internalised shame shows up in all kinds of ways, and not always in ways you'd immediately recognise.

We probably don't consciously go around thinking we're not worthy of love, but perhaps we feel the need to make others happy and be the reliable person that everyone can turn to, the one who always puts their own needs last. Or maybe we never ask for help or show weakness, because we are afraid people will think less of us if we do. Maybe we say yes to things we want to say no to, because we worry that we won't be liked or that love or respect will be taken away.

All these things, and many more, that we think are just quirks of our personality are in fact driven by feelings of shame that we have picked up along the way. The shame tries to protect us by making us work extra hard to cover up any weaknesses and flaws that might lead to further feelings of shame. But, as you'll know if you experienced any of these ways of living, it's *exhausting*.

## So, what's the point of shame?

Psychologically, shame is the feeling of humiliation, embarrassment, guilt, and/or self-consciousness that we feel when we think we have acted in a way that is wrong or believe we have failed in some way. It can also arise from comparing ourselves to others, either through our own observations or having it pointed out to us, which leaves us feeling that we are somehow lacking and makes us feel unlovable. Psychotherapist Joseph Burgo explains in his book *Shame: Free Yourself, Find Joy And Build True Self-Esteem* that the four most common causes of shame are: unrequited love, unwanted exposure, disappointed expectation, and exclusion (being left out).[5]

Most of us will have experienced at least one of these, but more likely all of them, at some point in our lives – I know I have. But it begs the question: why do we have shame in our emotional makeup? What's the point of something that is potentially so damaging to our sense of self-worth and wellbeing? Surely we'd be better off without it? It seems counterintuitive to say we need shame in our lives, but as I thought about it more, I began to wonder if it serves some evolutionary purpose and can even be good for us in some ways.

A lack of shame or feelings of accountability means there's nothing to stop us behaving in a harmful or selfish way, with no sense of social responsibility. So, this deeply embedded emotion plays a huge role in keeping us alive as a species by encouraging us to follow rules, play nicely, and live together harmoniously, as we social beings need. Without any shame there'd be chaos: we'd all be shouting our mouths off whenever someone annoyed us, ostracising or harming people (or worse) for being different, taking what isn't ours just because we want it – that kind of thing. The fact that the world appears to be overrun with – and in some cases ruled by – people who behave precisely in this way makes examining the idea of shame (and shamelessness) compelling.

## Weaponised shame

Shame can also be used to control us in negative ways. While "community shame" is commonly used to nudge us into conforming for the greater good and safety of us all, it can also be used to manipulate and control. Ever since humans realised that this horrible feeling of not being good enough can be spun, those in positions of power have always used it to their advantage. It doesn't have to mean shaming on a grand scale; being belittled by your boss so that you'll keep your head down and do as you're told is using shame as a weapon, you just may not have seen it that way.

On a larger scale, out of the office and into the big wide world, shame is used so regularly in our day-to-day lives, in things we experience subliminally and otherwise, that we don't really notice it anymore. We are so used to our perceived flaws being pointed out with one hand, with solutions to "fix" them with the other, that we don't register what's happening. The trillion-dollar beauty industry is built on and survives by weaponising our deep-rooted insecurities, combined with our genetic need to fit in and be accepted by our tribe. Beauty and unattainable eternal youth are seen as the pinnacle of power, and it takes a pretty robust sense of self-belief to withstand the pressure to look perfect and not buckle under the shame of not being so. And as no one can ever meet the goal of perfection because there's no universal definition of it, it's a perfect stick to beat us with.

In the 1990s and 2000s, it was common to see unflattering paparazzi photographs of famous women stamped with "The Circle of Shame", highlighting cellulite, sweat patches, or rounded bellies for the reader. The magazines that featured these photos would then run full-page articles on how to get rid of cellulite or get "beach body ready", alongside unachievable airbrushed images of women looking fabulous and adverts for the lotions and potions that promised to erase flaws. The premise was clear: don't look like these dishevelled women who sweat and wobble, or everyone will laugh and find you disgusting. Look like this instead, and everyone will love you!

During this time, I was a young woman in the public eye going through a divorce. Half-truths and misinformation had been printed about me on the front pages of newspapers, while reporters rifled through my bins and hid behind walls to take unflattering photos of me in my misery. I felt like I deserved all the pain that this public shaming brought, because I had done something wrong. I had a very brief affair as my deeply unhappy marriage was ending, and unbeknown to me someone sold the story to a national newspaper. I held my hands up and admitted it – and took the full hit of public shaming.

It felt like the whole world was judging me. That obviously wasn't entirely true, but we all know what it feels like when we are going through any kind of disgrace or shame; it feels like everyone knows, and everyone is talking about it. Some people say that those in the public eye should shrug off negative headlines, that it comes with the territory and shouldn't be taken so personally. But the headlines led to reactions in real life. I was spat on in the street by a neighbour. "Not so clever now, are we?" she snarled, and walked on. I was so overwhelmed with shame that I became agoraphobic, only leaving the house to go to work. I couldn't eat, because I felt I didn't deserve to enjoy the taste of food in my mouth. I felt I didn't deserve *anything* good, because of the shame I'd brought upon my family.

I didn't think I would ever feel anything other than shame, humiliation, and self-disgust. But eventually I did. Things calmed down as the newspapers moved on to someone else, and my life gradually went back to normal. Until the next time, when I failed again for another reason and the shame cycle repeated itself once more. And the next time. And the next. Each time was different, and I will touch on them as we journey through this book, but all carried their own pain, and their own lessons.

## Simultaneously universal and unique

So, if shame encourages us to hide, why have I decided to write about it and share my experiences so publicly? I am in my mid-50s, and I know what's coming. I know there will be fallout, and haters, and people deliberately getting the wrong end of the stick and enjoying my misfortune – all the things that come with shining a light on something that many would prefer remained in the dark. I have written about other experiences I have lived through and then researched, including trauma, burnout, and fear, and I know that it is helpful to talk about things that most people would rather we did not.

My personal experience right now is of excruciating shame because of financial ruin, which is a first for me. And somewhere inside my stressed-out brain it made sense for me to investigate this feeling, and to understand why we have it as part of our genetic makeup.

Shame is a universal experience. Shame doesn't care who you are, what you do, or what your bank balance or social status is. It's something we all feel.

But at the same time, shame is an entirely individual experience.

While shame is something we all *think* we understand, our unique outlook on the world means that what *I* think of as shameful, humiliating, embarrassing, or guilt-inducing is going to be different to what *you* think of these things. We may be talking about the same thing, but we are doing it with wildly different points of reference and perspectives. What might to one person be no biggie can be crushing to another: being fired from a job, having an affair, even not looking conventionally attractive. We are complicated beings, and no more so than when it comes to what causes us shame.

It's for this reason that it's important that we don't try to shame-compare. Just because *we* don't feel a sting when people act in a certain way or when we experience a challenging situation, it doesn't mean that everyone is as robust in that same circumstance. By the same token, just because we feel hurt or humiliated by someone's triggering behaviour doesn't mean that everyone else must view it in the same way. Understanding this helps us break out of our own private cycle of shame narrative.

Throughout my shameful experiences, I have not just learnt what shame feels like – horrible and debilitating are two words that sum it up nicely – but importantly, I have also learnt how it shows up. For me, shame has an insidious superpower: it convinces me that I am either unlovable, unlikeable, mad, bad, stupid, ugly, or a useless failure. It tells me how utterly worthless I am. But once I am able to recognise that voice for what it is, I can begin to challenge it.

My first challenge is: am I punishing myself for not being good enough? As the quote at the beginning of this chapter says, "Guilt says what I did was no good, shame says *I* am no good." Shame can occur when we turn a screw-up into an "*I* am a screw-up" mentality.

## Own your mistakes

One of my favourite quotes, which is why I began this book with it, is from the actress and producer Salma Hayek, who said, "If you did something wrong, don't let anybody take your mistake and use it against you. It belongs to you. It's yours. Own it."

We often forget that we can choose to see our mistakes as simply that – mistakes – and claim them before anyone else can weaponise them against us. There is no self-victimisation here, just pure ownership.

When I first heard the quote, I was thinking about my own financial failings and the shameful fallout to follow. It made me realise this: *you cannot be shamed if you refuse to accept the shaming.* Easier said than done, of course, which is one of the reasons I decided to write this book: it is my attempt to own my mistakes on a public scale, and in doing so let them remain just that – my mistakes – and not a source of shame for others to heap on me or me to heap on myself. Once you own your mistakes, refusing to let them be internalised as shame, it can give you the strength to get up and go again. And perhaps it's when we realise that we *all* make mistakes and none of us is perfect that we can truly begin to recognise, own, and conquer shame.

I was aware that I was hiding away, hoping that people didn't find out the mess I was in, because I knew the fallout would be horrible and I didn't feel emotionally robust enough to cope. I knew that I would be judged, looked down on, and probably

Shame is a universal experience. Shame doesn't care who you are, what you do, or what your bank balance or social status is laughed at. But then I realised that I would *never* feel emotionally robust enough to deal with it if I kept sitting in the dark, hoping no one would find out.

Living with the secret shame of failure and debt was far more insidious and damaging to me mentally and physically than standing up, shining a light on all of it and telling the world, "I have messed up. There, I've said it. I tried something and not only did it not work, but I have also lost everything. I am trying to make it better, but what's making that harder to do is the engulfing feelings of shame and embarrassment. And I don't want to live like this anymore."

I started by admitting the truth about my situation to a few people, and I was shocked by their response. "Me too," they whispered. I suddenly saw that, because shame makes you keep quiet about whatever it is that you feel bad about, you think you're the only one going through it. My whisperings to friends about my financial situation made me realise that so many people are closer to the edge than I thought and yet continue to try and "keep up with the Joneses", not knowing that the Joneses are doing the same thing.

I realised I was gripping onto my shame so tightly, while simultaneously *wishing it would release me*. I had to be the one to let go, to set it, and myself, free. And the only way I could do that was to throw open the curtains and let it fizz and dissolve in the light.

It took me a while to get there, and my story gets much worse before it gets better.

So, strap yourself in. Here. We. Go.

# Lessons in Becoming Shame*less*

1. **It's Not Just You**
   It just feels like it. Shame is a universal experience, even if it is uniquely felt and experienced by everyone. Take comfort in knowing that you are not alone, are not the first, and will certainly not be the last, to go through this.

2. **You Are Not the "Thing"**
   You're just experiencing the thing. Once you understand the difference between *making* a mistake and *being* the mistake, your world will feel lighter. The philosopher Descartes famously said, "I think, therefore I am", but we have somehow twisted that to believe it means we become the thing we think about. In particular, the thing that we are stressed and worried about. You are not stupid, you just might have done a stupid thing, and there is a difference. You still need to clean up the mess that the stupid thing has left behind, but *you are the one cleaning it, you are not the mess.*

3. **It's Your Mistake, So Own It**
   Hold your head high. Yes, you messed up, but again in the words of the utterly fabulous Salma Hayek, "So what? It's my mistake, not yours, you have your own."[6] Find me someone who has never done something they regretted, and there you will find someone who has never truly lived. The world will chatter about you regardless; whether you try and fail, try and succeed, or do nothing at all, so own your actions. The reaction to this, both good and bad, very often has little do with you.

2

# TIMING IS EVERYTHING

*When Things Don't Go to Plan*

*"In fashion, as in life, the right thing at
the right time is the right thing. The right
thing at the wrong time is the wrong thing."*[7]

Tom Ford, Fashion Designer and Filmmaker

In December 2020, when I told millions of people that I needed to be brave, to know whether I would fall or fly, I genuinely thought I stood a good chance of succeeding. After all, I'd had a successful career so far, had many strings to my bow, and I'd be partnering up with people who knew a lot more about running a business than I did. And yet, my lack of flying skills mean that I am now on the brink of ruin. So, how did I get here? Like most of life's big challenges, it happened slowly and then all at once.

The business I quit *Loose Women* for was called This Girl Is On Fire. It had started naturally when I began a blog back in 2018, then had grown into an online magazine where I invited experienced journalists, authors, and specialists to write articles packed with helpful advice for women in midlife. We covered everything from dealing with the mental and physical symptoms of the menopause to coping with divorce, deciding on career change, dealing with blended families – all kinds of things. It was an organic success, read every week by hundreds of thousands of women from 80 countries around the world; I was receiving messages from women in Europe, Australia, America, Canada, and India. It was wonderful to know I was helping so many women. It was free to anyone who needed it, but it was *not* free to run.

## From blog to business

I had been funding the blog myself through my main job – being a presenter on television – and brand work. I refused sponsors and advertising because I wanted to keep it clean, so that everything the women saw was from an expert and was purely helpful.

In 2019 my husband Nick and I decided to add an e-commerce component to the site, to promote female-founded businesses that offered products or services that helped women in some way. This made more sense to me; rather than just accepting a fee from a big brand to put a banner on my site, I would be helping female entrepreneurs as well as visitors to the website. It was like a "Not On The High Street" (the site for small creative enterprises to reach a wider market), but offering products and services needed by women, provided by women. I loved setting it up, knowing that my profile was helping small businesses get traction they would never normally get. We included coaching and mentoring for the businesses that came on board, which was especially helpful to kitchen-table startups, and also offered a supportive community to more established female founders.

It took months to put together and get us ready for launch. In early Spring 2020 we were excited; the appetite was there, the suppliers were ready, and we were all set to press go. And just as we did, the global coronavirus pandemic started, and the world went into lockdown.

Our timing could not have been worse. Global shipping issues meant that containers filled with products were stranded and orders couldn't be fulfilled. It also meant that many of the products and services offered by the businesses we housed, such as online fitness and wellbeing classes, were now being given away for free by higher profile competitors who could easily absorb the cost. It had an immediate impact on our business, as we lost over 50 per cent of our female entrepreneurs overnight because they were unable to trade.

It was awful. We had invested time and money into getting the platform up and running, and it became abundantly clear from the messages we were receiving via the blog site that it wasn't just our distraught female entrepreneurs who needed practical emotional support during the pandemic – most of our site visitors did, too.

We decided that the best way to help the women, and keep our business going, was to create a membership. Women would pay a small monthly fee to be part of a community who all wanted to learn how to cope with anxiety, stress, and life challenges and feel good about themselves mentally, physically, and emotionally. They wouldn't be "sold" anything; once they joined, they had a rich bounty of things to help and support them in every possible way.

I knew that helping a woman with her emotional and mental growth wasn't simply about personal wellbeing or relationships. It would also help her have the strength and resilience to progress in her career or in her entrepreneurial journey. So, we pivoted. We trained as life coaches, doing a mixture of online and in-person sessions (when Covid restrictions allowed) and used this to put together the best packages possible. I ran masterclasses on overcoming fear, self-sabotage, and building self-belief and better relationships, and Nick offered one-to-one and group mentoring to help them overcome specific personal or professional issues.

I passionately wanted women to feel supported and encouraged while they built their toolkit of skills. I interviewed incredible experts for masterclasses and our podcast, both of which were hosted inside our This Girl Is On Fire app. At this stage we were using a white label app – a ready-made platform that you can customise – which is a more cost-effective way to test and measure what you are offering, and to see what gets traction, what's easy to use or not, that kind of thing. We really wanted to create our own bespoke app that worked exactly how we needed it to, but this would take time and money, and we needed to test it first before going all in.

The women we served *loved* what we brought to them, and I loved what I was doing. But I needed the business to grow so that it could support itself without relying on my personal financial input from other work and my savings.

Hindsight is a wonderful thing. It is all so obvious now that I should never have used my own savings and credit to support my business. I took out loans and partly remortgaged my house, fully believing that once it was a success I would be able to pay everything back. I was so wrapped up in what I was creating that I ignored letters and emails telling me that the time to pay back had begun...

And so, one year after we'd had to pivot our marketplace business into a purely coaching business because of Covid, there came a knock on the door. I opened it to find a very large man standing on my doorstep. I instantly knew who he was and why he was there. He was a bailiff.

I had never met a bailiff before, but I'd seen them in movies. Bailiffs were huge scary-looking men who came into your house and took your stuff because you were pathetic and weak and borrowed money or spent more than you should have.

This man was formidable rather than scary, but I could see the pity in his eyes when he said, "Are you Andrea McLean?" The blood rushed in my ears, and I tried not to cry and throw up. "May I come in?" I had no other choice; I let him in, and one hour and a few cups of tea later he left, and we put the house on the market.

The debts were paid off, and we reframed the whole experience: yes, we had made mistakes, but they weren't going to define us. We now had a clean slate, ready to start again and continue building our business, and now with some cash in the bank from the sale of the house to do it. We settled into a rental home and went full throttle into making our business work. I fully believed in what I was doing; I believed in myself, and in Nick, and felt that a cash injection was just what we needed. In hindsight, I should have asked for support from experienced investors who offer funding and expertise to startups in exchange for equity and not put my personal savings on the line *again*. But I did, and that was my second mistake.

We paid tens of thousands of pounds to join groups of experts who could help us grow the business. These were in-person and online meetings, which provided advice to help entrepreneurs build their businesses and network with others in similar positions. We had a business mentor to guide us. We hired a company to build an app that would be better than the white label one we were currently using and be better suited to our needs and ambitions. There was no investment money coming "in", we were paying "out", for everything.

They say, "When it rains, it pours", and it's true. This is the moment when *everything* started to go wrong.

## Failure to launch

The launch of our app was delayed by over a year due to every conceivable kind of tech hiccup. Our money was going down, but I persisted, following different paths that led nowhere, each time met with a shrug from our business mentors, mutterings of, "Hmm, it normally works, you must be doing it wrong" – and an invoice.

As the launch time drew near, we decided that we needed to make as much noise as we could and paid a PR company to help orchestrate an incredible launch day. We gathered every expert I had interviewed, every influencer and celebrity who had been part of our journey or had supported us in some way, plus members of our community. At 8pm, Nick and I walked on stage in central London to metaphorically press GO to make our incredible app accessible to the world. Our interview with the wonderful journalist Emma "Guns" Gunavardhana was to be live streamed across all our socials, where journalists who couldn't make it in person were invited to watch and report.

The first problem came when I raised the microphone to my mouth to speak. Feedback howled out of the speakers and the audience winced and put their hands over their ears. I paused, then carried on. It screeched again, and I could hear my own voice looping back with a delay. I looked over to the sound engineer, who was frowning and staring down at his equipment. Simply carrying on and hoping no one would notice was not an option, so I acknowledged the problem and asked if he needed a moment to sort it. He shook his head angrily.

I started again. The microphone shrieked, the audience winced, and the room was filled with my own voice echoing back. I decided to keep going, in case he needed to adjust the levels and perhaps it would settle down. It didn't.

Our whole broadcast to the world was horrific, and the impact of the launch was lost. We came off stage, outwardly smiling and mingling with our lovely guests who had come from all over the UK. We had photos taken, answered questions from the assembled press, and grinned until our faces hurt, but inside I was raging.

The next morning, we checked the app, excited to see how many new members had signed up. None. Not a single one. Cue the nausea and whooshing in the ears. My heart was pounding so hard I could see it.

The whole thing had failed to launch. I was devastated.

Why? Timing…

In 2022, Google changed its rules, ending support for older systems so forcing developers to reconfigure logins, storage, and interfaces, or face non-functional apps. Stricter Data Safety laws also required detailed disclosure of data collection, and even making mild wellness claims like "feel better" risked rejection. Meanwhile, Apple launched App Tracking Transparency, massively reducing the effectiveness of Facebook and Instagram ads, and introduced privacy labels with strict wording requirements: we were among countless to be rejected for getting this wrong.

Both Google and Apple demanded in-app purchases go through their systems, costing developers a 30 per cent fee. Our small startup struggled to keep up, relying heavily on one incredible woman on our tech team while launching. Many others faced similar challenges, and research suggests that direct-to-consumer businesses saw revenue fall by 60 per cent during this period.[8]

## Time for some Ugly Truths

Nick and I were due to go on a family holiday the following week. The plan had been to get our breath back after all the hard work leading up to the launch, and return feeling refreshed and ready to hit the ground running. Instead, we drove to Italy in a thick internal fog of fear. It was his 50th birthday and we'd hired a villa for the whole family so we could celebrate his milestone along with our business finally turning a corner.

It was a disaster.

Our family had its biggest ever falling out to date. With a combination of emotionally charged behaviour that will be familiar to anyone parenting teens or young adults, and simmering tensions between us, the whole thing exploded. Every issue that comes with being a blended family erupted. Anyone who has met and married later in life, as we did, bringing with them their own children and hoping that all sides will blend together seamlessly, will have experienced this. Sides were taken. Tempers lost. Words said. Tears shed. I was so angry I got into our car and drove off, something I would never normally do, because I *cannot* drive on the other side of the road. I turned right from our villa and just kept going for an hour in a straight line, too scared to go anywhere complicated.

Eventually I got to a roundabout and turned back, only pausing to pull over and google flights home. I was going to take my daughter Amy (my son hadn't joined this family holiday, something he's probably grateful for now) and leave the rest of them in Italy to fight among themselves. I'd had it with everyone. I got back to the house to hear the argument still going, only now I could hear my name being mentioned. I sat quietly and listened to what was being said about me, until I had heard enough. *We all need to talk.* I texted Nick. *Time for some Ugly Truths.*

Ugly Truths is what Nick and I call our conversations that need to happen, but which we know will mean someone will be hurt. We gathered everyone around the kitchen table, the young adults and teens with sulky tear-stained faces, and gave everyone their chance to speak, the only rule being no interrupting. Everyone had their say. The atmosphere was heavy, but the conversation was good.

Ugly Truths had been given light and air, and the chance to be recognised and redeemed. The kids headed off to their rooms to lick their (mainly self-inflicted) wounds. Nick and I went to ours to *really* have it out. We had the kind of talk we couldn't have in front of the kids. Some real home truths that were *beyond ugly* needed to be said. The holiday ended earlier than it was supposed to because we called it a day.

On the return journey Amy was very quiet and slept on the back seat through most of Italy and France. It turned out she had hepatitis, likely caused by dirty water. Because, as if career and family crises weren't enough, now we had a health crisis to add into the mix. She ended up in hospital back in the UK for three days, where I slept on a camp bed next to her. Weirdly, it gave me respite from the stress of the business not working and the family fallout. Amy being ill brought the rest of our lives into sharp focus.

Health has a way of doing that, doesn't it? Often, we can be so concerned with our finances or our own success until something threatens the basic things that we should all be so thankful for, like our relationships and health. Thankfully, Amy was finally given the all-clear, but then it was my turn to be humbled by health: I got my third bout of Covid.

## The breaking point

The first time, Covid had felt like the flu. The second time was the same, but because we were so up against it with running the business, I carried on working from my bed. But this time was different; I was wiped out and I couldn't think straight. My whole body ached, not just my joints but my muscles and skin. I developed painful sores inside my nose that wouldn't clear. My hair started thinning on the top and sides of my head. I couldn't walk more than a couple of paces without having to stop and rest, and I felt on fire inside, and so weak. The joints in my hands felt stiff and sore, and my palms were red and hot. Everything hurt. Two weeks went by without improvement. Then three, then four, and then five.

I tried to keep going, but I couldn't. I lay in bed either sleeping or stressing about everything I couldn't do, knowing that it was all piling up without me. The webinars I'd written and set up for my community were too much for me to do, so Nick had to host them. But that wasn't what people were paying for; they were paying for *me*. I couldn't do any extra work to keep the money coming in, something that had been our staple for the past few years. No brand work or endorsements meant the offers slowly dried up and went elsewhere.

Weeks turned into months, and it became clear that this was not something I was going to bounce back from. I managed to do a couple of classes over Zoom to honour a programme I had put together for my members, but when the last one of the series finished, I said goodbye to them, smiling and waving so they would never guess how awful I felt, and closed my computer.

I walked into the kitchen, looking smart from the waist up in a blouse and with makeup on, but in my pyjama bottoms, slippers, and a blanket from the waist down, and said to Nick, "That's it. I'm done."

We were almost out of money and had no way of making any unless I got better. It was costing us around £20,000 a month to run the business, paying for tech and our team of freelancers and experts. Our loyal members had stayed with us during the bumpy ride from our white label app to our bespoke one, and after the initial "failure to launch" we had gained some more as they trickled in each month, but not enough to fully cover costs. We had never paid ourselves; every penny went back into keeping the business afloat.

Nick had sold the properties in the portfolio he had built up over 20 years to put money into our pot. I had borrowed everything I could from my presenting business and from my personal savings, and it was almost all gone. We sat down and tallied up everything we owed, and what we needed just to survive. It was not good. I had always believed that I would be able to pay myself back, and now it was clear that was not going to happen. Both my presenting business and This Girl Is On Fire were going under, and I was about to be in debt on two fronts, both personally and professionally. I had some personal savings left, which kept us going for a short while, but I owed money to my presenting business, having taken money from one business to support the other, and now I had no way to pay it back.

We paid our team and gave everyone notice that we were folding. It was sad, so sad. I felt a weird kind of numbness and disbelief that it was really all over. It was heartbreaking, as everyone who worked for us believed in what we were doing and liked being part of something special. We had all hoped that we were going to go on and do great things. But we were just one of millions of startups that fail. As the ones who had enlisted these wonderful freelancers, who all had families to support just as we did, Nick and I both felt wretched that they would now have to look for new work.

And so would we. We wrote a list of people we could reach out to, and over the next few weeks spent hours contacting them and asking for work; even though I didn't know how I'd actually be able to *do* the work as I was still ill, I had to try something. The answers were all the same; nothing right now but keep in touch.

Eventually I had to swallow my pride and ask for money; the shame was unbearable.

## Crash landing

I reached out to someone I had known professionally and personally for many years. They had become close friends of ours; we had stayed at their home, been to their children's weddings, and had come close a few times to going into business with them but the timing had never been quite right. I stumbled when they asked how I was, and then eventually crumbled. I told them what was happening, and that I was sorry and embarrassed to ask, but was there any way they could help? I offered to work in whatever capacity, but I needed to be paid, not just given a "trade swap", which was how we normally did business. They listened and were kind, saying they would have a think and get back to me. In the meantime, they offered to give me some money up front that I could work off. Relief flooded me. It was all going to be okay.

But then a week went by, and nothing. And then another.

I didn't want to be pushy, but I really needed the upfront payment and to know what they'd like me to do for them in exchange. I had texted, then emailed, and then eventually rang, which made me feel sick. "Don't worry," I was told, it would happen. They were about to launch something that we had almost worked together on years before, and they still really wanted me to be a part of it. And yes, they would get some money over to me soon. They said they loved me. That I was like a daughter to them. I was family.

I breathed out. I was worrying about nothing. It would sort itself out. I was still concerned about whether I would be well enough to return to full-time work again while I still felt so ill, but I pushed it to the back of my mind. Of course I could push through, I'd done it before and I could do it again. This was too important.

Then I got a call from my agent. A big brand that I liked was offering me a six-month contract, for a great fee – it was a life saver, hooray! I called my friend to say we'd been given a lifeline and explained what the job was. Oh no, they said. This was too similar to what they wanted to do with me, only it would be a long-running thing, not just for six months. They told me there was no way I could do this job and then work with them. I had to choose.

Six months work now and a lifeline of money that would help us while we figured out our next steps? Or a longer-term job with people I knew, liked, and trusted? It was agonising. I chose them.

They were pleased and said they'd be in touch with details very soon.

Another week went by. And then another. By now we were running on fumes. My calls were now being ignored, as were my texts. Then came a message I'd hoped for. *Could we have a meeting at their office in London?*

I knew I didn't look my best; I was still ravaged by the after-effects of Covid, but I was determined to be as shiny and sparkling as possible. Nick and I sat in their office, and for the next fifteen minutes just listened, numb with disbelief. Everything was off. No money, and no working for them. They'd had a meeting with their investors, and it had been decided that:

*"Your star has faded, Andrea. You don't have the value you once did. You don't have the star quality we need. What you need to do is get a job on TV again, and then we can have another chat. Okay?"*

These are words that have haunted me ever since. *Your star has faded*.

I was no longer airborne. I had officially fallen.

\*\*\*

It's a strange feeling reliving those awful moments.

"Timing is everything," they say, and oh my goodness, are they right! Who could have factored in a global pandemic arriving exactly as a platform helping small businesses was launched? Or tech giants changing their setups as a small personal growth app launched? Or turning down a much-needed job, only to have your other offer of work and security withdrawn?

What I can see now is that there were many factors at play that caused the financial mess we ended up in: bad timing at several key points created huge ripple effects that we could never have foreseen; getting Covid so badly that I took months to recover and couldn't work; being let down by advisors and friends.

But the shame of admitting things were going wrong, and that we'd made some bad calls, also paralysed us into inaction. We'd kept going on the same course and hoped that something magical would happen to make our problems go away. Unfortunately, life doesn't work like that, as I discovered too late and got to the point where I was in horrific debt.

You can hobble along for an extraordinarily long time on the brink of failure without anyone knowing; it's something many of us do and is simply a way of life. It's not fun, it's very stressful, and if you are one of the unfortunate ones who through bad luck or bad choices tip over that edge, you discover how quickly things can change.

## Sinking into debt

The reasons why we end up in debt are rich (every pun intended) and varied. For me, my business failed for a variety of reasons, and then I became too ill to earn money to keep funding it, while working on the issues that all startups have as they find their feet. For others, it might be that they have lived beyond their means or didn't reduce their outgoings when their incomings started shrinking. Or maybe the cost of their outgoings increased, and increased again, until they found themselves foundering.

This is a situation so many of us found ourselves in during the pandemic, and the fallout has continued long after: mortgage increases, bills going up, savings going down, and systemic changes in the world requiring nimble adaptation to new norms that don't always fit your line of work. At the time of writing, according to a report by The Money and Mental Health Institute, around 5.2 *million* people in the UK are currently behind on credit payments.[9] Debt is all around us.

I have experienced failure in every aspect of my life, but *nothing* compares to how I felt finding myself in debt. The same report states that 50 per cent of people who are behind on payments have felt suicidal.

There is a shame that comes with being in insurmountable debt that is hard to articulate; a feeling of weakness, of not being good enough or smart enough as those who are not. There is also grief, a sense of loss for what you had and worked so hard for. There is anger, as you try to climb out of a hole that you dug yourself into and cannot, no matter how hard you fight and struggle, get out of. There is a deep despondency as hope finally dies.

Before we move on, there is something that I want to be clear about. This is what my experience of debt feels like to *me*. I don't know what it feels like to anyone else who finds themselves in debt, and I am not for a second suggesting that my experience is the same as someone who finds themself enduring abject poverty. I completely appreciate that there are people in the world with far greater problems than mine.

I can only speak of my experience as someone middle aged and middle class who finds themselves in debt. I had, through my work and earnings, managed to live a comfortable life in a nice home in a good area, with personal savings and a private pension. I went on decent holidays with my family and drove a good-quality car. I had a safety net, a buffer between me and debt which made it feel like it was something that happened to other people, not me. Until it did. It is rarely spoken about, because you don't want anyone to know just how close to obliteration you really are. Among those I *have* spoken to who are in the same situation as me (and there are more of us than you'd think), to the outside world everything looks fine – in fact, it looks good. But behind closed doors there is choking panic.

Where do you begin, when you have left it too late? When your bank account is running on fumes and you didn't adjust your lifestyle, your business structure, or at the very least your outgoings, until the day you cannot pay a bill. So many of us leave it too late because we believe that "something will happen to make it better". It has to, because the alternative is too awful, too shameful. Something will happen to save us from this, and then we can all go back to normal, and one day we will laugh and raise a wry eyebrow at how close we came to disaster.

But nothing comes.

## Trying to stay afloat

You manage to avoid going out with friends for a while by feigning "busyness", and thankfully their genuine busyness means that the texts asking for a date for coffee or dinner get fewer. But *are* they genuinely busy? Or are they in the same position as you and neither of you are talking about it? This means you don't have to spend any money on socialising, which is a financial win, plus you don't have to lie about how you're doing, which is an emotional one.

Middle-aged, middle-class debt is in its own Tupperware container of pain. Oh, the shame of it. Of not quite managing to keep up. Of not being as smart as we thought. The side eyes and the whispers and the new WhatsApp groups that are set up without us, so that our predicament can be dissected and discussed freely, like a modern-day version of Lady Whistledown's scandalous newsletter in *Bridgerton*.

If it was in a Netflix drama it'd be funny. But it's not. It is happening in your home, which is a rental because you've already sold your house to pay off the first round of debts and re-invest in your business. But that didn't work, and now you can't afford your rent because you haven't earned any money in five months, but you also can't afford to downsize again because a new landlord would need to see your accounts… and your bank account is overdrawn.

You've tried to take control by arranging for payment freezes on the bank loans and credit cards you used to try and stay afloat, but they are about to start again. You've tried to give your lease car back, but they won't accept it without a balloon payment because you haven't had it long enough. But you can't afford the balloon payment because the bottom has fallen out of the second-hand electric car market, which means even if you can sell it, you won't get enough money to cover the payment.

So, you tell the finance company you can't afford to pay for your car any more as you need the money for rent and bills, and you cancel the direct debit and spend sleepless nights worrying that someone (possibly another bailiff) is going to turn up on your doorstep and collect the car you have tried to give back but they won't take. You worry about whether this would be a bad thing or a good thing; what would it mean?

You have sold some of your furniture and are selling your clothes to go towards your rent. You have tried to sell your engagement ring, but jewellery shops know why you're doing it and only offer you a small fraction of what you paid for it, even with the box, the receipt and paperwork. So, you still have it, but for how much longer?

You are now half seriously considering setting up an Only Fans page for your feet, as they are the only part of you that hasn't sagged under the weight of stress and middle age. Lily Allen did it "ironically", so maybe there is a market for it? You are looking drawn and tired, but you can't afford a facial, so you pretend you prefer to look "natural" and "age gracefully". You also can't afford to get your nails done any more, so tell people you are "having a break, as all that gel kills your nails, you know".

You are struggling to afford the weekly food shop, but you don't qualify for benefits as you aren't *quite* broke enough. You can't tell anyone that you can't sleep at night and spend all day applying for work, any work, while trying to appear casual and not at all desperate, because they will smell it on you and give it to someone less, you know… *needy.*

If this sounds horribly familiar, then my heart goes out to you, and I know exactly how you are feeling.

The first time I spoke to a debt collecting agency on the phone about my financial situation, I cried. I was embarrassed and ashamed that I had got myself into this mess again, and the man was utterly unmoved and unhelpful and made me feel disgusting.

I cried the next time too, but this time because the lady on the phone was nice to me. I was relieved that she didn't know it was me, "that lady off the telly", because that would have been even worse. But the fact that she was kind to me, just some random woman in debt, made me feel better. Even though she couldn't significantly help, I felt less alone – she told me she was getting lots of calls like mine. I don't know why the fact that other people were in the same situation helped, because I hate to think of anyone else feeling this way, but for some reason it did.

I have always thought of myself as a kind, compassionate person, but I realised that when it came to me, and my situation, I was judging myself harshly. It felt like I was the *only one* who was struggling. I know, what an ego, right? But don't we all do this when faced with something challenging, whether it's debt, illness, or a failed relationship? I found it easier to feel sympathy for other people who had got themselves into this situation, and discovering there were many more like me helped me to have compassion for myself.

## Why you should panic early

Most of the time we don't want to look too far ahead because it's too scary, but not looking at something doesn't stop it from getting worse if it has already begun. If there is one *huge* lesson that I have learnt from my experiences, and if I can pass one thing on to you, then it is this: don't let shame stop you from panicking early.

Panicking early is looking at what plans you will put in place if something happens – like installing fire doors to stop the flames engulfing your whole house. And above all, you *must* stick to them, even if you're thinking, "Oh, but if I just keep going a tiny bit longer it will all be fine!" That way madness lies. And I was the queen of keeping going for "just a little longer" and refusing to see how bad things were.

While failure should never define you and become internalised as shame, it's a wasted experience if it doesn't *teach* you something.

I know I am hugely resilient. I know I have grit and determination. These are great qualities that have got me through (and are still getting me through) some tough times. But they can be an Achilles heel because I am too ashamed to admit when I have got something wrong, so I have to keep going to make it right. I see that now.

Shame, secrecy, and inaction go hand-in-hand. We can label it as resilience, because that sounds good, but is it really? Or are we too afraid to tell anyone that we have gone so far down this road that we have no idea how to pull back from it, and we'd almost rather die than face the shame of people knowing we have made a mistake. Because once we tell someone, we have to face the fact that it's reality: we have completely messed up.

I didn't tell a soul what we were going through at the time, and only started to open up about it to very close friends when we had to move house again because we could no longer afford the rent on the one we were living in. I was ashamed that I'd been so stupid. It was easy to hide away; I was ill and didn't want to socialise anyway, and people were understanding. In the months that followed, when I eventually ventured out and went to friends' homes for lunch, I discovered that more people are in precarious financial situations than they would have you believe. It was quite a shock.

People who seemed uber successful, who went on great holidays, or drove nice cars, or lived in nice houses, whispered to me that every month they were on the brink of it all collapsing around their ears, and it would only take a couple of months of their income stopping for them to fail like I did. I was not alone. I was just one of the unlucky few who actually teetered over the edge.

I minimised our experiences to all but a close few. I've been pondering over why that is, and I think the reasons are layered. Yes, there was shame – especially among friends who are successful and living the exciting life that I used to before I couldn't afford it anymore. But I knew that *real* friends wouldn't make me feel ashamed; they love me and want me to be okay. A lot of the reason was because I didn't want them to feel sorry for me. I just wanted them to understand that I couldn't join in on a lot of the fun stuff that costs money, like going out to dinner or on holiday, but their time and company and having a laugh were free, and I could afford that.

## Going public

We all know that in theory the first step towards feeling better about your situation is to share your shameful story with loved ones in private. That's one thing. But owning our shame publicly feels like something else entirely.

It was only recently that I shared anything publicly about my business failing and about being in debt. I was invited to give a keynote speech for International Women's Day in March, in front of around 500 businesswomen and entrepreneurs. I know, right? Me, giving a talk to successful entrepreneurs – go figure. It had already been a challenge; I was still unwell and recovering from another health episode.

I'd had the flu that was doing the rounds before Christmas, and at first just thought I had it badly. I didn't want to make a fuss, so took to my bed and kept out of the way. But, after finding me collapsed in the bathroom, Nick rang our GP and was told to call an ambulance immediately. I was rushed to A&E, where, after a lot of prodding, poking, scans and X-rays, I was informed that I had acute pneumonia, kidney failure and sepsis. I spent five days in hospital, after which I had to return daily, then weekly, to be attached to an antibiotic drip. I wasn't fully discharged until March, and still felt weak and pretty awful, but I wanted to honour my commitment to speak at the International Women's Day event, not only because I don't like letting people down, but also it was a paid gig and we needed the money.

I spoke for half an hour, around the theme of "Changing Identities". It was about how, as women, we are born and identified as someone's daughter, sister, and friend, and then become someone's employee, boss, wife, and mother. Our identities are so often defined by our relationship to others and rarely simply about who *we* are, just as ourselves. This can be comforting at times, as it shows we mean something to someone. But when our identity changes – whether through divorce, job loss, or debt, either through our choices or through no fault of our own – it throws up unexpected challenges. If we are no longer that person, who are we? I spoke about my various identities: I was that girl who arrived in the Midlands with a broad Caribbean accent, then I became that weathergirl, then that Loose Woman, then I became a "Didn't you used to be…?"

As I talked about my life's learnings, I realised I couldn't leave this part of my story out. So, I said it out loud. "My business went bust, and I lost everything. I can now add 'failed entrepreneur' to my list of identities, alongside daughter, sister, wife, TV presenter, and author."

The room fell silent, and I could feel the shock that I was owning up to something so personal. We are used to hearing things like this from multimillionaires who talk about their "first" business failing before they figured out what to do and went on to become rich beyond their wildest dreams. But not so much from someone who has had it all and lost it and is still clawing her way back.

As I said the words, I could feel myself choke with emotion. But strangely, *the emotion wasn't shame.* I felt proud of myself for owning it. Saying the words out loud, in a public forum, is an act of incredible vulnerability, and it's completely understandable why we don't want to do it. It can make us feel horribly self-conscious about our shortcomings and there is a real fear that we will be ridiculed and rejected by our peers and by strangers. It's tough.

That day the response was incredible and inspired me to speak out more. Women rushed up to me afterwards, telling me that they had been moved to tears, because no one talks about the shame of failing and the struggle to keep all the balls in the air. The organiser contacted me afterwards to say there had been great feedback, and everyone enjoyed hearing my story. What a relief, from a room full of people who were clearly succeeding where I failed.

When it comes to failure and associated shame in our work life as opposed to our personal life, there is a disconnect. We can laugh and empathise with someone whose home life is a mess; let's face it, most WhatsApp group chats and Instagram influencers would be lost without someone making a hash of their love life or parenting. There is an acceptance about it that allows us to laugh at our mistakes, and chalk them up to experience. This doesn't follow when it comes to work; understandably, because the stakes are high and we have mortgages and bills to think of, which I can personally tell you are no laughing matter when you can't pay them.

We all think that everyone else knows what they are doing, and that we are the only ones who are messing up.

But we aren't, we just don't hear about the failures, we only hear about the successes. No one *wants* to repeatedly fail, but when we do (and we will!) we always have the chance to learn from it. Your friends probably do this to you in your personal life, gently remind you of past mistakes so you don't repeat them. But if a workplace has the kind of environment where you are

We all think that everyone else knows what they are doing, and that we are the only ones who are messing up.
But we aren't, we just don't hear about the failures

*positively* reminded of past efforts that didn't go well so that the same mistakes aren't repeated, then it also saves face and a bucketload of shame. It means that there is less embarrassment about owning your mistake; remember – it's yours, don't let anyone take it from you! If you don't have anyone to hold you to task or remind you, then keeping a note of everything you have tried and failed at will hopefully stop you from over-excitedly going full steam ahead, potentially into another failure.

Learn from my mistakes, if not your own. Because, well, when it comes to out-failing the competition, I can safely say that right now, I am an industry leader. But what does an industry leader do when it all falls apart? She applies for a job in Starbucks...

# Lessons in Becoming Shame*less* About Things Not Going to Plan

1. **Hindsight Is a Wonderful Thing**

   There is no point in wishing you had done things differently. It's done. Now what can you do? I wish that my timing had been better when I started my business, but it wasn't, and that I made a thousand different decisions, but I didn't. You will have your own moments in life where you feel embarrassed or ashamed about decisions you have made or actions you took – we all do. Looking back is a useful exercise if you are willing to learn from the outcome of the decisions you made, but if you are just ruminating and feeling shameful about your past then it's pointless. It doesn't help you, and it certainly doesn't change the outcome of whatever you did. So now you know better, what can you do better?

2. **Sometimes Ugly Truths Need to Be Said**
   Whether it's in our career, our relationships, or our financial situation, no one likes hearing things that make them confront their actions, especially if it brings up feelings of anger and shame. But sometimes it needs to happen so that situations can be resolved. We all tell ourselves stories that fit the narrative we are working to in our heads, and we forget that those stories are not always true, or helpful. Have the courage to have difficult conversations and recognise that any resulting anger and deflection is almost always rooted in shame and can provide valuable insight. It shines a light on feelings that have lurked in the darkness of our mind and allows them to be seen clearly from a different perspective, which helps to set them free. Have the ugly conversation – especially if it is about the state of your finances – and work together on easing the problem.

3. **Panic Early**
   Taking action is better than being forced into a reaction, so DO SOMETHING! This feels at odds with what we are told about striving hard for success, but it's the truth. Looking ahead and seeing what's potentially going to happen, especially when we don't like what we see, is *hard*. It's why we'd rather bury our heads in the sand and keep going. Taking steps so you are either ready for a situation, or can avoid it altogether, is simply redirecting your energy in a positive, productive way. Reach out, ask for help, advice, and, if necessary, financial support. And most importantly, *take it*.

# 3

# "YOU CANNOT WORK IN STARBUCKS"

*The Shame of Failure After Success.*

*"It is not the critic who counts; not the man who points out how the strong man stumbles, or where the doer of deeds could have done them better. The credit belongs to the man who is actually in the arena, whose face is marred by dust and sweat and blood; who strives valiantly... who at best knows in the end the triumph of high achievement, and who at worst, if he fails, at least fails while daring greatly."*[10]

Theodore Roosevelt, 26th President of the United States

"I'd stack shelves if I had to," says the famous woman across from me.

We're talking in an abstract way about work ethic and providing for our families, and of being the breadwinner. She looks glossy, shiny, and successful, having just come from a photo shoot.

I nod. She makes it sound easy, I think, but it's not. Because, having worked in TV, the second you get a job stacking shelves, someone will take a snap of you on their phone, and it'll be on social media in seconds. Then it will be in the online press and the weekly magazines, with headlines like: "How the mighty are fallen: once-successful TV presenter is now reduced to stacking shelves." And then you risk never getting a job on telly again. So, it sounds easy in theory, but in practice it's hard.

## Contemplating reinvention

"You CANNOT work in Starbucks," said my agent, when I told him I had applied.

I knew he was thinking about the mobile phone snap, the online chatter, the newspaper reports and career-ending shame.

But what else could I do? If there was a bottomless pit of opportunities, I found myself standing on the floor of it, staring up at unscalable walls. It was September; a year and a half since I'd had to close down my business. I'd had to borrow money off my parents and my sister to pay our bills. Nick had asked his family if they could help us pay our rent.

There had been *some* work for Nick and me during this time, which had hugely helped. I had been approached by a female entrepreneur who asked if I'd create a media coaching programme for her community. I'd never considered doing anything like that before, but I said yes, and put together a masterclass. She loved it, and it sold well, which kept us going for a few months. This inspired me to recreate the same kind of thing for other female entrepreneurs and their communities, and for a while it had worked, as I could work from home at my own pace.

Then things had dried up again, despite our efforts. The jobs for me, the coaching clients for Nick... nothing materialised. For either of us.

I had woken up again after another night of stress-related dreams. My jaw was throbbing after clenching all night, and my teeth hurt. I was now genuinely afraid that they were going to fall out because I clenched so hard. I had actually bitten through my night brace; it was worn down to holes where my back teeth connected, and I had cracked a tooth. I hadn't been to the dentist for almost two years as I couldn't afford it, and the broken brace behind my top teeth was so weak I could feel it jagging out.

I needed a job.

Not just so I could afford to go to the dentist, but so that I could breathe.

I had put myself "out there" on LinkedIn and had been scouring Indeed, the job-searching equivalent of Tinder. Only no one was swiping right for me. Not one single coffee shop. Was it because I was a 55-year-old woman who had no practical experience in anything useful? Possibly. But still, there must be *something* that a faded TV presenter could do, which paid more than minimum wage and wouldn't end up with me being featured in the sidebar of shame.

I had somehow become Moira from *Schitt's Creek*, without the wigs or fabulous wardrobe.

*Schitt's Creek* is one of my favourite TV shows. I watched it during lockdown and fell in love with each and every one of the characters. But I happened to catch an episode recently and found myself too choked up to enjoy it in the way I used to. It was the final episode, where everything had come good – when someone believed in them again and they felt worthy, that they had value in the world and a purpose.

I cried when I watched it, because that was the worst part about what I was experiencing. It wasn't just the choking, clenching stress of not being able to pay my bills and worrying about supporting my family. It was feeling like I didn't have any worth or purpose.

## When the world moves on without you

I have friends my age who have found themselves staring into the same abyss. The world is changing at such a rate that many in their 40s and 50s have found their industries fundamentally altered and their skills obsolete. Being an expert with years of experience doesn't guarantee anything anymore. This isn't something that will go away; younger generations are also going to experience the next wave of turbulence in the job market with the increasing implementation of AI. Times are changing for all of us.

But right now, my generation are finding themselves on the stinky end of a modern Industrial Revolution: not financially in a position to stop working, but unable to replace the work that has disappeared because we are seen as too old to adapt.

According to the Office for National Statistics in 2024,[11] older workers (who are classed as aged 50 and above) are more likely to experience "economic inactivity" than younger workers. Some

I had somehow become Moira from *Schitt's Creek*, without the wigs or fabulous wardrobe of this could be because of early retirement, and for those in that boat I say, fair play and best of luck to you. Or it could mean ill health, in which case, but for very different reasons, best of luck to you, too. But the main reason for over 50s not being in work is because of a horrible Catch 22 situation: once you are out of work, it's hard to get back in, and the longer you are out, the less employable you become.

Somehow, in life's game of snakes and ladders, we have found ourselves at the bottom of the pile again. Whether it's through a career break to have children, redundancy, ill health, or – like me – you quit your job to follow your heart during the "Great Resignation" of 2020, and it didn't work out, and now you have a gap in your resume and no idea how to start again.

Statistically, workers over the age of 50 are more likely to be classified as long-term unemployed compared to younger age groups. Data from Age UK and the Office for National Statistics indicates that those over 50 who are out of work for a year or more may face up to a 50 per cent likelihood of remaining unemployed for several more years.[12]

Why? Here's the kicker…

Far too many employers seem to perceive long-term unemployed older workers as being "irrelevant" and having "outdated skills", which leads to reluctance in hiring.

We are not talking about senior citizens here; I'm talking about people the same age as Reece Witherspoon (49) and Cameron Diaz (53). You don't have to be a Hollywood legend to still be relevant, do you? To have a wealth of experience and be kick-ass smart enough to figure your way around a new IT system?

Surveys show that older job seekers in the UK often encounter age discrimination during the hiring process. A study by the Centre for Ageing Better[13] found that older candidates often feel sidelined during recruitment, facing *assumptions* about their adaptability, productivity, and digital skills. Not facts – assumptions.

Of course, economics has to play a part, and this is where us so-called oldies really feel the kick.

We cost more. Why? Because we have worked for 20, sometimes 30 years and have built up a lifetime of skills and experience which are reflected in the salaries we have been paid. Our greater experience contributes to increased productivity and fewer mistakes, and we often have invaluable industry knowledge and strong soft skills that take years to develop. We also have bills to pay and families to support – many of us have Gen Zers living at home with us, barely paying any rent, and are coping with the financial strain of supporting elderly parents – so our financial needs are often greater. It's not greed or entitlement, it's simply fact.

In a fast-changing world it's difficult to know how best to adapt. Automation and streamlining have always caused alarm and fear, but as a species we have always learnt how to lean in and adapt to go with the new flow. But now, at this moment in our history, it's hard to grasp what we are supposed to adapt *to*.

The image that keeps coming to my mind is of Robert de Niro in the film *The Intern,* where a sweet, retired 70-year-old wants to feel needed and useful, so he applies for and is taken on as an intern by a harassed Anne Hathaway in her cool online fashion store. He is out of touch, charmingly out of date, and everyone laughs at him behind his back. Until, of course, he uses his soft skills and life experience to save the day, and everyone loves him.

That feeling of still wanting and needing to contribute, but no longer being seen as "useful", or even "cool", is something that is hard to explain unless you have experienced it.

Your star can fade in any industry; maybe you worked hard and rose through the ranks in your company, but cutbacks have been made and you weren't selected to stay. At the other end of the scale, and I'm aware that this doesn't apply to many, maybe you were in a band that used to sell out stadiums, then the world had a change of musical taste, and you're not wanted any more.

What are you supposed to do then?

I remember, years ago, there was a news story about a former successful band member who was snapped by paparazzi while selling burgers from a van outside a football ground. How the press laughed at him. *Oh, how the mighty are fallen*, they sneered. *From touring the world to flipping burgers*.

Think about it, though; we wouldn't sneer at anyone else who sells burgers, so why do we do it when someone has been successful elsewhere? Surely the shame should lie purely in the hearts and actions of those passing judgement, not the people being judged.

## Through the looking glass

But what do you do when no one wants you? When you are still *you*, when you are still great at whatever thing it is you do, but no one wants it? No one *wants* to be the pop star selling burgers. No one *wants* to be the faded TV star. No one wants to be the redundant manager, or office worker, or stylist, or designer, or any number of jobs that have changed beyond recognition in the past ten years.

Perhaps you took a career break to raise a family and have never managed to get back to where you were; now you're feeling left behind because things have moved on and you can't catch up. Maybe you suffer from crushing anxiety, which has taken your confidence, and you don't feel able to do the job you once did because it has changed so much since you started out.

Our circumstances change, and there should be no shame in that. Things happen that are good, bad, and ugly. Getting caught up in how other people might react, or view you, or think about you, or talk about you, is beyond your control. It's impossibly hard not to worry about it, but it honestly is the only way through.

One of my favourite quotes on this (and if you've been reading my books for a while, by now you will have noticed that I love a quote and a retro film reference) is by the American sociologist Charles Horton Cooley.

"I am not what I think I am. I am not what you think I am. I am what I think you think I am."[14]

You'll have to read that a few times to let it sink in.

He theorised that our ideas around who we are and where we stand in society aren't judged purely through our own thoughts, feelings, and experiences. In his book *Human Nature and the Societal Order*, he put forward the idea that our sense of self is formed in two ways, not one. Our sense of identity comes from both our actual experiences *and* by what we imagine other people's thoughts are about those actions. He called this the "looking-glass self", proposing that we see ourselves through the eyes of others without ever truly knowing what their view is.

How often have we allowed our shame about our sense of self, our fallen status, or our feelings of being "less than" bubble up to the surface because we believe others will think poorly of us? Maybe they do, and we know this because they have told us to our face or through social media, or the usual way, which is behind our backs, and it's filtered its way to us. But maybe they don't, and we have allowed our view of who we are to be dictated by what we *think* they think of us.

There are so many trip hazards when it comes to getting through life's ups and downs, and overthinking ourselves into paralysis because we worry about how we will be perceived is part of it. On the one hand, it is a sensible thing to do because misconception has consequences. On the other, it is impossible to know exactly how something is going to play out; you can only make an educated guess and then decide what to do – or not do.

## Haters gonna hate

Here's the thing. People will talk about you anyway, whether you try something and wildly succeed, or fail horribly, or even if you just lie on the couch all day. So, you may as well do what you want, or what you have to. Unless their opinion pays your bills and feeds your kids, they don't count. Unless they have something helpful to say because they have experienced what you have, they don't count.

The list of people whose opinion of me I care about is very small. Of these, I either love them or at least like them very much, respect all of them, and know they have my best interests at heart. I have met them all in person, and some I am related to. This might be a useful way for you to figure out whether someone who is giving you a hard time is worthy of your attention and your emotion.

I started this chapter with the quote by Theodore Roosevelt, the 26th President of The United States, for a reason: he tells us not to listen to those criticising from the sidelines but not actually doing anything. The only person who counts is the person struggling and trying their best, getting back up time and time again after defeat. Because even if they failed, at least they failed while bravely trying.

This is an important fact to remember in these days of keyboard critics who can attack from the shadows, anonymously or from a distance, or even the mums at the school gate who have mastered the art of stage whispering and side eye. The critics may form a deafening chorus, "pointing out how the strong man stumbles", or laughing at a former pop star selling burgers from a van, or a former TV presenter working in a coffee shop, but their opinions *do not count*. I couldn't even *get* a job in a coffee shop when I most wanted it, and I would not have cared less what critics thought. And, by the way, your loss Starbucks; I'd have been a *great* barista.

This is what we all have to remind ourselves of when our fortunes change. That there is *no shame* in falling, or failing, and doing what you need to do to get back on your feet again.

## Struggling to focus on solutions

This kind of positive reframing is so easy to do when life is going well. But when my business went under and I found myself in unimaginable debt, while being sick with Covid and later hospitalised, I found it more and more challenging to do. As my fitness plummeted because I was too exhausted and sick to push myself, it became increasingly hard to be motivated and positive about my situation. I became downright miserable and depressed. Everything hurt, life was hard, and there was no getting away from the stress of it all. There was *a lot* going on.

I couldn't reframe. What the hell was the point, when all I could see were the walls of the hole I was in, and my mind whirled trying to solve these problems and climb out? It was exhausting, and I was exhausted.

It was something that my husband and I completely disagreed on, and it caused a huge rift between us at the time. He became irritated and angry with my low, disagreeable mood. I felt hurt and misunderstood and unsupported, because he just wanted me to snap out of it.

Nick had an incredible ability to block out anything he didn't want to think about, simply calling it "unhelpful". I didn't understand it at all; how was his head not filled with our long and scary list of problems? He shrugged when I asked him, and his answer was always the same: "It's not helpful to stress about the problem, so I don't, otherwise I will spiral. I can only think about the solution." While I would lie in bed for hours with every possible worst-case scenario whirling around my brain, he could fall asleep within seconds of his head hitting the pillow. When I eventually slept, I dreamt about my teeth falling out, running for trains and missing them, annoying my old boss, and needing the loo but every toilet cubicle I found was filthy (like *Trainspotting*-level dirty) and had no door, so everyone could see me. I was even shamed in my sleep.

I was intrigued about our different responses to our loss of financial security, so I investigated whether it impacts men and women differently. I discovered that women often *do* react differently to financial loss compared to men,[15] with a 2024 poll by

US data centre Bankrate revealing that this is significantly linked to their need for safety and security.[16] Of course, both men and women experience stress and anxiety around money, but research suggests that women's emotional and behavioural responses to financial setbacks are often shaped by a deep-rooted need for stability, security, and long-term safety.[17]

There are many reasons for this, not least biologically, as women are prone to being more risk averse because instability can affect dependent children, but they are also socially encouraged to "be careful". For me, add into the mix my experience of financial loss because of my previous divorces, and the feelings of emotional instability and not feeling "safe" that brought, it wasn't surprising that I was feeling wobbly.

One research paper I read said that, for women, when it comes to money worries, as well as feeling stressed, depressed, and anxious, they are more likely to have a stroke, heart attack, or develop diabetes. And on top of that, being under financial duress *makes you put on weight*.[18]

FFS. As if it's not hard enough.

Reading this actually helped, as it allowed me to let go of the fear that I was just being a Debbie Downer and getting chubby round the middle because I was annoying and lazy. No, I was demotivated and sad because I was biologically programmed to react in exactly this way during prolonged periods of stress. Doing this research really helped me put aside my shameful feelings of not coping as well as Nick seemed to be. But then I still had the problem of what to do to change how I was feeling.

The internet is awash with information about how to get your finances back on track when you have come apart at the seams. But to be honest, most of the articles made me angry. They spoke loftily about creating a savings pot and an emergency fund of around six months' savings, and of keeping an eye on your credit score. This is great advice if you are Panicking Early, and I would very much advise that you do this if you are in a position to. But

I was not. I had to use every single penny that came in through the door just to stay afloat. I was selling anything that wasn't pinned down to pay for groceries, so the idea of a savings pot prompted a bitter shake of the head and muttered expletives.

I did find two places that were hugely helpful; the financial journalist Martin Lewis and the advice he shares about debt via the Money Saving Expert website, and Laura Pomfret and her Financielle website. Both gave me practical helpful advice that made me feel less of an idiot and eventually helped me manage my debt, for which I will always be grateful. I've added their details in the resources at the end of the book in case you are in a similar situation and could do with some practical help.

## Nothing left to lose

One thing I became aware of, and which provided the financial and emotional breathing space we desperately needed, was that I could apply to cash in my private pension on my 55th birthday. This was something I'd been putting money towards since I can remember and was supposed to keep contributing to until I was a ripe old age before enjoying. I never thought I'd be cashing it in early and therefore losing almost 40 per cent of everything I'd saved to tax. But we needed the money *now,* to live on. It wasn't the windfall I was building towards, but it hugely helped. So that October, I applied and waited.

That was one thing I was able to do that released some pressure. The second thing I did was leave my husband.

Not forever (although I must admit there were moments when I thought about it). I removed myself from my stressful environment. I booked a very cheap flight to visit my sister in Northern Ireland and spent a week flat-sitting her parents-in-law's beautiful apartment overlooking the sea. I slept. I ate. I walked. I sat on the stony beach, wrapped in my duvet coat and beanie, and watched the wind-whipped waves. I meditated – something I used to do but had gotten out of the habit of – and did some gentle yoga.

I spent time with my sister and her family, and she kindly booked me in for some reflexology, reiki, and a facial. I ate chocolate and drank wine, and I didn't have to explain or justify my actions to anyone. I did exactly what I wanted for a whole week. I also did a lot of writing. I wrote down how I was feeling about my life and was brutally honest. I let it all out and took a good look at it, feeling sad that I'd had to cope with so much. Reading it as if it was someone else made me properly see just how much I'd been carrying, and that it was no wonder I felt so ill, and tired, and fed up. Bloody hell, it had been a tough few years.

Stepping away from things for a while works, and it doesn't have to mean a month-long, five-star stay in Bali, although that sounds seriously lovely. Flat-sitting my sister's in-law's place was free. If you want to step outside of your life for a while, just to give yourself the headspace to think clearly, ask around. Even if friends are just going away for the weekend, see if you can stay in their empty place for a couple of nights. I didn't realise how much I needed to do this until I did it, and I'd urge you to do the same. There is no shame in admitting you need time on your own and doing it for free.

I'd also hugely recommend writing things down. It gets it all out of your system in an honest way, because, let's face it, we can be far more ragey when we write stuff down than when we are sitting opposite the person we are feeling ragey about. It also helps you see things more clearly when you look back on it, which helps you gain the compassion for yourself that you'd so easily give to someone else.

On my second-to-last day, Nick rang. We didn't talk about how awkward and strained things had become between us and how upset we both were with each other; that's not his style, and I had got used to it by now. I knew we would sort things out eventually, in our own strange way. His terrible habit of dealing with it was, once he felt that things had settled down, he'd talk about it in the past tense and say something casual like, "God, remember that time when... yeah, I didn't handle that too well." And that would be his apology for being an absolute shit.

It was fine. My own terrible method of sorting it out was to go into emotional, laborious detail, and poke our almost scabbed-over wounds until they bled, and then find a way to make it all his fault, because, well, wasn't it? So, *not doing* either of those terrible things worked fine for us in this moment, because deep down we both felt exonerated, and knew the other was trying to make things better in their own warped way. We were sure everything would blow over because we loved each other – even if we didn't particularly *like* each other right now.

Anyway, that's not what he rang to talk about. He rang to say he'd been thinking, and what about if we just sold all our stuff, literally *everything we owned,* and used the money to go to Spain and live? The lease was almost up on our London place and so we needed to move anyway. The kids were making plans of their own, so this would just speed things up a bit. Amy, my youngest, had just been accepted into university in Spain, so there'd be no guilt about going there and leaving her behind. We obviously wouldn't go to the same place as her – that would be weird. My son had gone travelling, with, it seemed, very little intention of coming back to grey, damp England. Nick's daughter had been living with us to save some cash but was almost ready to get a flat share in London. In a few months we officially didn't need to be stationed anywhere for the kids.

Nick had investigated, and we could live in Spain for less than it cost in London in terms of rent and basics, and they had a Digital Nomad remote working visa system that meant we could stay for up to three years. It was six months since we'd had to borrow money for rent, and although we were still in debt, things were at last improving financially. My pension had come in, and Nick had built up his client list again and was working as a consultant for a couple of companies. I worked from home anyway, earning most of my money through brand work, which I could do at my own pace. We could get cheap flights back when we needed to for coaching, speaking, and event hosting jobs. In theory, with the wind in the right direction, there was a chance this could work.

I didn't even blink. "Yup, sounds good. I just want to keep my favourite Christmas decorations. Everything else can go."

And I meant it. The past couple of years had reduced my attachment to "things" to zero. Okay, 0.5 if you include my love for my Christmas baubles. Everything else was just *stuff*.

We spent hours checking out flat rentals in Spain. It was the first time in a long time that we both felt excited by something. We had spoken for years about moving to the sun and had looked at all different parts of the world, but the timing had never been right. But maybe, just maybe, it was finally right now? It was a crazy idea, but what do you have to lose when you've already lost everything?

It didn't cross my mind to wonder what anyone would think of us doing this, because it wasn't anyone else's business. To paraphrase Teddy Roosevelt, why the hell not? If I was going to fail, I may as well fail while daring greatly, and in sunshine.

# Lessons in Becoming Shame*less* About Starting Again

1. **It's Not Your Fault You Feel Awful**
   But you do need to take action. I am making a huge assumption, based on my own sexuality and relationship status, that you are a woman, possibly in a relationship with a man, and I absolutely take on board that's not necessarily the case. However, knowing that men and women often react differently to financial stress and challenging times means that what works for them won't necessarily work for you, so bear

this in mind if you are a woman getting advice and support from men in your life. You need to feel safe, as this is where most of your stress is coming from. Find your own way to practically reframe and work through your experiences in a way that makes *you* feel good. If doing what your male partner does isn't working for you, then don't keep going just to keep *the* peace, do what works for you to find *your* peace.

2. **Get Some Distance**
You can't fix your problems with the same mindset that caused them. Sometimes the best thing you can do when you feel overwhelmed, stuck, angry, and depressed is to change your environment. Getting away from the place or the people that are making you feel stressed is the first step away from the problems themselves. Of course, you will take a lot of them with you: they are in your head, after all. But changing your environment, even just going away for a weekend or staying with a friend, helps you to change your outlook.

It gives you the chance to breathe out, and to see things from a bird's-eye view rather than looking up from the bottom of the abyss. It helps you identify solutions, and it gives your poor body and brain a rest from all that cortisol. This stress hormone affects every part of you, not just your ability to think clearly and react calmly, so anything you can do to lower it is a good thing. It doesn't have to cost much or be a big deal to really help. Have a think about who you can ask to facilitate you getting away for just a moment; who can put you up, and who can hold the fort? You almost certainly have more options than you think.

3. **What Do You Have to Lose When You've Lost Everything?**
Shameful thoughts about what others may or may not think about our actions is what holds most of us in a state of

inaction. Whether it is getting a job in a coffee shop after having a big fancy career or selling everything you own and moving to another country to start again, shaping your own narrative is much more important than worrying about how others see your choices. In other words, if it feels right and works for you and your loved ones, don't worry about what anyone else thinks about it – especially if it doesn't impact them.

# 4

# BEHIND THE SCENES

## SCENES

*When Shame Shows Up At Work*

*"There's no business like show business."*

Irving Berlin, Composer and Songwriter

Put a group of people together and let the magic happen. That's pretty much the remit of any workplace. With television, it's a place where magic really does happen. However, like any show that glitters and shines, what happens front of house is rarely the same as what happens behind the curtain.

For over two decades, my place of work was a live television studio, somewhere that broadcast content that informed and entertained to the nation. I *loved* it, from the first heady moment when I stood in front of the camera, the red light came on, and I just had to do what was expected of me and keep going, even if I was so nervous I forgot what to do with my hands or what my name was. It was scary, exhilarating, and exciting all at the same time.

There are so many moving parts to making a TV show look effortless; from the floor crew operating cameras and microphones and lights to the gallery team calling out timings, setting up shots and instructing presenters and crew, and the producers and researchers who come up with incredible ideas and work tirelessly to make them a reality. When you are watching a TV show at home, you only see the very tip of the iceberg of what it takes to put it together; much like anyone going to the theatre only sees the performers onstage and doesn't give much thought to those involved in the fantastic script or beautiful set and lighting, without whom they'd just be looking at people pretending to be other people, and it wouldn't be very impressive at all.

There is a team spirit that comes with working in TV that can only be likened to theatre, film, or any of the creative arts. The chaos of pulling it all together and making something shiny and impressive for the public is addictive. But, like any playground full of fun, brightly coloured things, it also has a jagged side that catches like a splinter on a swing.

## Navigating hierarchies and double standards

As someone who'd had lots of other "normal" jobs before starting her career on telly, I already knew what it felt like to work alongside or underneath someone who either threw their weight around or was deliberately difficult. I, like many of us, experienced it when I was working in bars, hairdressers, shops and offices. It's tough, and while you just have to swallow some things and chalk it up to the rich and varied human experience we all share, sometimes it's more than that.

Working in television is no different. Except…

How to explain?

Working in television is a bit like being in a nursery where some of the toddlers get told off for having tantrums, and others get sweeties and teddy bears.

As a fellow toddler, it doesn't make much sense, because you always thought that kind of thing was "bad", but here in this special place, where everyone on the outside seems very excited and impressed that you are here, the same rules don't seem to apply.

Working in
television is a bit
like being in a
nursery where
some of the
toddlers get told
off for having
tantrums, and
others get sweeties
and teddy bears

The first time I witnessed this was when I worked in breakfast television. Obviously there was a hierarchy, as there is with every job, but it gradually became clear that some people could get away with throwing their toys out of the pram and others could not.

It wasn't always obvious who would be able to get away with certain behaviour; sometimes it was long-standing "talent" (that's what the presenters were known as), or it could be a favoured director or producer. Like any business, I suppose it came down to how valuable an asset someone was to the show. "Not valuable" meant you'd be out on your ear at the slightest whiff of anarchy. "Very valuable" meant you could pretty much do whatever you wanted, to whoever you wanted, as long as you didn't do it in public.

As a young woman who came from a traditional working-class family where you were always polite and grateful to whoever hired you, this was a revelation. Weren't they scared about getting in trouble, or fired? Apparently not. I was more afraid of what my parents would think if I'd ever behaved that way and lost my job than I was of anyone in charge.

Did I ever experience bad behaviour directed at me? Of course I did; everyone did. Casual and targeted misogyny was rife in the 1990s and 2000s, and the usual response was simply to smile, internally rage, and *find another way* to make it work. Unless of course you couldn't, so you smiled, internally raged, and took it until you found another job. Because, as my old boss used to tell me any time I went into his office to challenge something that didn't seem right, "See that box of tapes? That's people who would do your job for free. Anything else?"

This was what he told me when I came back from my 12-week maternity leave after the birth of my first child, which is the longest you can risk taking as a freelance presenter otherwise someone else will appear in your absence, you will be forgotten about, and you'll lose your job. I discovered that my hours in my role as both a weather and features presenter, and therefore my pay, had been halved. The reason, I was told, was that now I'd had a baby, he didn't feel he could rely on me as much so wasn't going to use me as often. No discussion, no reasoning, just me standing in my boss's office with him looking at me like: "Why are you still in here?"

I didn't react, at least not in front of him, even though I wanted to. I'd had an emergency C-section during a horrendous birth experience and was juggling a colicky baby and post-surgery complications with the need to be back at work, behaving like everything was exactly the same as it was the day I left. As the breadwinner, my husband and I needed my salary to be as it was before my brief maternity leave, but I didn't feel like I could challenge the decision when he told me my hours had changed without consultation or warning.

It's an interesting dynamic, now that I can look at it from a distance. Women are so often shamed and penalised for being "too emotional" in the workplace; I'm sure we have all had times when we have cried in the toilets or welled up during a combative exchange with a colleague. I know I have. We know that emotions are what makes us human, and that we are simply humans performing a task in exchange for a salary so that we can feed, clothe, and house ourselves. It's really that basic. And yet, when we enter the place we work in, the emotional side of our human "being" is expected to be left at the door. What's the solution? How do we feel our emotions in a way that means we don't have to pretend to be robots from the second we clock in?

## Finding ways to make it work

My solution was to learn how to negotiate. Don't go in with a problem; go in offering "another way", one that benefits the workplace first and foremost but also helps me keep my job.

And so, I put forward ideas and said yes to anything that came up. I didn't talk about the juggle, because no one did. I never mentioned *anything* that might have been seen as a negative; every request, even the difficult ones, was met with: "Absolutely. No problem." And I found a way; it was simply all I could do back then, and I am very grateful that I was able to make it work.

Every woman who goes back to work after having a child must think on their feet when it comes to workplace dynamics. It's something that the incredible broadcaster, author, and campaigner Anna Whitehouse has been discussing and championing for over a decade, after she was forced to leave her job as a senior copywriter because her flexible working request was denied. The reason? That it would "open the floodgates" to others. To put this into perspective, Anna had requested to arrive 15 minutes earlier in the day, so she could then leave 15 minutes earlier to pick her daughter up from nursery. For the sake of 15 minutes, Anna became one of the 54,000 women every year who lose their jobs because their workplace can't accommodate the needs of working mothers.[19]

In Anna's case, it fired her up to change an outdated working system that shamed and penalised women returning to work after having children. A decade later, and "Flex Appeal", the campaign she started to push for flexible working, has finally seen the introduction of the Flexible Working Act, which means that every employee can request flexible working as soon as they join a company.[20]

In my case – while getting divorced when my son was a toddler, moving home, finding childcare that as a single parent meant I could drop everything and be sent to the other side of the country with an hour's notice and stay overnight (a regular occurrence when presenting the weather on breakfast television) – my answer was always the same: "No problem." And I figured it out, with the help of my sister, who moved in with me for the first year, and my mum, who flew in from Africa (where my parents lived during this part of my adult life) to help me when needed. I then had a lovely young au pair from France called Emilie who lived with me for 18 months (and we are still in touch).

Later, my biggest champion came in the form of Lin, who became my much-loved "other mum" (as I called her) for 17 years. She began working for me when my daughter was only a few months old and my son was five, and I could not have managed childcare without her. She became part of my family, and long after the kids no longer needed her, I still did as a wingman, sounding board, and friend.

I most definitely didn't do it alone, and I am still grateful that I was able to have such great people in my corner; not everyone can. With all that support behind me, I worked my way up the ranks to become a stand-in anchor on the breakfast show when one of the co-hosts was away.

## Six cameras and no safety net

My first time co-anchoring a show was utterly terrifying, and to be honest I only said yes because I appreciated that they had put their trust in me, not because I thought I could do it. I knew I could present on live television; I had years of experience in doing that, but co-hosting a live news-based breakfast TV show is a unique beast. If you haven't watched *The Morning Show* on Apple TV, starring Jennifer Aniston and Reece Witherspoon, then I'd urge you to. It is a brilliant depiction of what it's like working on a live news-based breakfast TV show (although their dressing rooms were *way* nicer than ours, with three of us sharing one tiny room at GMTV – though it was fun, like hanging out with schoolfriends between classes).

To me, my co-host was a tough, seasoned pro who appeared to have little time for what he considered to be "silly girls" trying their best. I was thrown in at the deep end, as most people are in telly, and knew I'd either drown in front of millions of people and never get the chance to try again, or I'd somehow doggy paddle my way through it until I got better.

On that first morning, I walked into the familiar studio as I did every day, but this time it was different. I was sitting on the hallowed sofa instead of standing in front of my weather map, looking at the room from a different angle. I now had six cameras pointing at me rather than one, a stack of notes and briefings on all the guests who we would be interviewing over the course of the next two hours, and a printed-out script, where I'd scribbled the pronunciations of the tricky surnames I'd have to effortlessly say. My co-host and I were allocated different segments to introduce and link to, so I'd made sure I was across my parts so there would be no surprises.

I didn't normally use autocue, because the majority of my presenting had either been live outside broadcasts where you have to memorise what you are going to say, or packaged features where I did many pieces to camera from different places, which were edited together. Or I'd be presenting the weather from inside the studio, where I had to memorise the information and describe what was happening while pointing to a green screen. I was a very experienced presenter – just not in this.

I felt stitched up within the first hour, as my co-host, who had barely seemed to glance at me since I sat down, read *my* link, leaving me to read his.

My heart flipped; what was he doing? I hadn't prepared *his* links – I didn't know what words I might stumble over. Sight reading had never been a strong point; I was the person who would stumble and stutter in English class if I had to read aloud a passage that I hadn't prepared. Now I was having to do it on live television, with millions watching.

It was my first lesson in how to become brilliant at reading autocue – a vital part of live studio presenting where a script scrolls up on a special screen in front of a camera. No one at home can see it, and it looks as if you are simply talking. I learned how to read many lines at once. The first sentence is the one I read out loud, but I scan ahead at the same time, looking for any difficult words that might trip me up, so that by the time I have to say them they don't scare me anymore. It also means that I know the tone of voice to use, because I can see that a gear change is coming. Reading ahead is like seeing around a bend when you're driving; you know what's coming so it doesn't take you by surprise, and you're less likely to crash.

After a few days of presenting together, apart from when we smiled into the camera and introduced ourselves and our guests, my co-host had hardly said a single word to me. During each commercial break he seemed to turn his back on me and read the newspaper, or chat to the director in the gallery, only turning back around and smiling as the theme tune played. During one of these breaks, I looked at him and said, "Sooo... I know this is all a bit strange, me doing this with you. How am I doing?" He glanced up from the newspaper and jokingly said, "F*ck me. I hadn't noticed you're here," and carried on reading.

Everyone in the studio heard and saw it. I felt overwhelmed by shame, and I felt my face go red. I looked down at my notes and prepared for the next segment, squashing down my feelings. Stop it. Not now. You're on telly. Smile.

The newspapers picked up on my nerves, and columnists ran bitchy articles about how young and inexperienced and "desperate to please" I seemed alongside my older, more experienced co-host. One even called me "The Most Irritating Woman on Telly".

Thank God for the production crew, who would give me a discreet thumbs up and flash "you got this" smiles to me.

By the end of that week, I was prepping for the whole show; I can't believe I'd been naive enough to think I only had to be across "my" parts. It meant I was ready for when my co-host decided to move things around and interview my guest instead of his, or when he took a link and made it his own. When an interview overran, I had to tidy up the mess by paraphrasing what I was reading off a moving autocue so that we made the commercial break in time, I could do it. I was still terrified, but I was getting used to the terror.

I was thrown in at the deep end, I doggy paddled, and then I learnt to swim. Would I have learnt as fast if I hadn't needed to? Would I have grasped that you must think ahead and be prepared for every possible worst-case scenario, including the ones where you are stitched up by your co-presenter? I doubt it, and I realised that my co-host did me a huge favour. As he pointed out to me later, once I had passed the test of our bumpy first week and we went on to have a friendly working relationship, a good TV presenter isn't paid for when it all goes right: you are paid for when it all goes wrong and you can handle it.

It's interesting to look back on times when we've felt ashamed that we didn't know how to handle something, whether it's at work or in our personal lives.  How much easier is it to feel compassion for our younger selves who were simply trying their best, than for ourselves in the present moment? Even though we know in theory that it's the challenging times that build character and resilience, when you are in the thick of it and you know you are out of your depth, it doesn't feel that way.

If we can find a moment to step back and allow ourselves the same generosity of spirit and compassion that we would give anyone else in this situation, it would most certainly take away some of the stinging shame we have all felt. I'm genuinely grateful for that challenging week standing in for the usual host, and even for my co-host's behaviour, because it made me a much better presenter the next time I did it, and the next.

## Earning my place on the sofa

In 2007, when I was offered the anchoring job on *Loose Women* at the same time as working on GMTV, things became more challenging. When I was approached to join the show, I initially turned it down because I knew how feisty it was, as years before I'd been a guest. But when it was made clear that I would be *the anchor,* that changed everything. I may not be pushy, but I am strong and fair and have always been able to see all sides in an argument, which is the skill an anchor – who must control the debate rather than jump in with opinions – needs to have. However, not everyone was happy with my appointment.

A few women had been tried out in the anchor role before me, and in all honesty were much more experienced than I was, so I could understand why they were angry. One, a powerful old-school newspaper journalist, thought my appointment was a joke, and, as she sometimes appeared on the breakfast news show where I was still working, made her feelings very clear. It was awful, and awkward, so I decided to nip it in the bud. I told her that I appreciated that she was angry, but she should be pissed off with management, not with me, because wouldn't she also have taken the job if she'd been in my shoes? We never became buddies, but she stopped snarling at me every time she saw me and bitching about me while I was in earshot, which was something.

To this day, I have no idea why I got the job over anyone else, but I'm grateful that I did, and that what started out as maternity cover led to me becoming the longest-serving anchor of a multi-award-winning show.

It's funny. I am probably the same age now that she was then, and I completely empathise with her rage at being replaced by someone younger, especially if it feels like that's the only reason you have been passed over. It sucks. It makes you feel old and past it, and that your years of experience count for nothing. It has always been this way, but it doesn't feel great when it's your turn.

You never forget the moment a shiny-eyed youngster turns to you at work and adds the immortal words "… for your age" at the end of a sentence about your skills, your looks, or even your attitude. It hits you like a ton of bricks that you are now *that* woman.

I have always treated people who are new and inexperienced with care and support, because I remember how it feels to be out of your depth. And yes, I have discovered the hard way that this kindness is not always reciprocated, as one young presenter I once worked with mistook my kindness for weakness and did her utmost to elbow me out of my job. Unlike the bolshy journalist who bitched about me to anyone who'd listen, my claws remained retracted, but my heels most certainly dug in, and I kept my job.

The first year of doing both the breakfast show and *Loose Women* was hideous. I was mentally and physically wrecked after having my second baby; I was in a new relationship that had its issues; I still hadn't fully recovered from my divorce; and my partner wasn't used to sharing a home with anyone, let alone a brand-new baby (ours!), an exhausted, post-partum, hormonal woman and a five-year-old. I had also moved house, so I wasn't close to my circle of friends. I was doing my original job of presenting the weather and features on GMTV, which meant getting up at 3am, and *Loose Women*, which involved hosting a live show and a pre-recorded show until 7pm. (When I joined, the show didn't go out live every day, two days were pre-recorded.)

But that wasn't the hard part; the hardest part was that *every Wednesday* evening I would get an apologetic call from the newsroom telling me that the weather segment was going to be "on the road" the next day.

Why does this matter?

Every Thursday I needed to be in the morning planning meeting for *Loose Women* at 8:45am. My last weather report finished at 8:30am, which gave me just enough time to whip off my microphone, grab my things and head downstairs, ready to start my second job of the day. All I requested was to be studio-based on Thursdays. One day a week.

But on Wednesday evenings I'd get the call saying I was going to be sent somewhere the following morning that was *just inconvenient enough* to make me late or miss the *Loose Women* planning meeting, and sometimes the script run through. There were times I arrived breathless and dishevelled into the studio to be mic'd up and have an earpiece shoved in my ear, and I'd run on and host a live TV show that I wasn't completely prepped for. Sometimes I'd be wearing the same clothes I'd rushed in wearing, my hair barely brushed, in front of a screaming, clapping studio audience and millions of viewers at home, with feisty panellists who needed to be kept to time and in line – and not all of them happy about who their new anchor was. Thank goodness for the "be ready for anything" training I'd had from my co-host years before.

It was a challenging juggle. And so, 18 months later, I quit the breakfast show to go all in on *Loose Women*. The production team there had been sympathetic and encouraging, and my years there ended up being both the happiest and unhappiest of times.

There are so many things that I loved about being on the show for 13 years: the brilliant discussions about things that were taboo elsewhere; the fact that there wasn't a single programme like it, where four women with different lives and opinions could sit and talk about issues from fresh and unique perspectives, giving women at home a feeling of being seen and heard. Nothing was off topic – we discussed everything from parenting challenges, cancer battles, alcoholism and abuse to sexy dreams, most embarrassing moments, and the silly things our children did. Rich and varied conversations, just like those that happen between women around the world.

The fun, the belly laughter, the nights out, and the trips away together were all wonderful. It took a while to feel accepted, but once I was, I felt like I had found my tribe. We were hugely popular: we won every award, the press found us funny, and the public loved us. It was an incredible thing to be part of, and I was fiercely proud of it and what we did.

And then, some years into my time there, it started to go wrong for me.

## Walking away without shame

One of the reasons was because of my style of anchoring the show. I was naturally quieter than the others, which to me made sense, as their job as panellists was to be feisty and have brilliantly opposing opinions. My job as anchor was to mediate and make sure everyone got to have their say and every argument was balanced.

For those who haven't seen it, *Loose Women* is a panel discussion show hosted by a main anchor, with three regular panellists plus a celebrity guest. There were normally around 14 women who were a rotating part of the show while I was there, and two anchors. This keeps the show fresh, allowing it to vary from day to day and for the audience to experience a different mix of personalities and opinions.

I never saw my job as being part of the panel and airing feisty opinions – although I had lots of them, I kept most of them to myself unless I felt they were helpful. I would sit in the morning planning meeting, and while I joined in the banter, I mainly listened.

The purpose of the meeting was to create the content and structure of that day's show. We would all have read the daily newspapers, and the production team would also have gone through weekly magazines, online forums, and anywhere else where interesting stories might come from. The producer would pitch ideas to see which got the best response from the panellists, and if it fell flat or no one had anything to add, we'd move on. Anything that sparked debate or prompted a personal anecdote was perfect. We would also pitch in ideas: from something that had happened at home, to a TV drama we were enjoying and how it related to us personally, to things that had caught our eye in the news.

I'd make notes from the to and fro of impassioned debate, so that once on air I could bring things up and keep the conversation vibrant, and so it didn't taper off, as sometimes the women would think, "Oh I've already said that" and forget they hadn't said it on air. It became clear that some of the panel didn't like how quiet I was during the morning meeting, and I was told by the programme editor that I needed to get more involved in the discussion.

I explained that if I was jumping in with my opinions and fighting my corner like they did, I wouldn't be paying attention to what anyone else was saying. I felt that my role was not to host the morning meeting like I hosted the actual show, that in the meeting the pressure was off, and thoughts and opinions buzzed freely around the room. My job was to get the best out of everyone *on air*, for our viewers, and to do that I needed to listen to all the opinions beforehand. But not everyone liked it.

Why?

Because some of the women thought I was going to save my "best anecdote" for the actual show and outshine them. I would watch them occasionally do it with each other – stealing a good punchline that someone else had said in the morning meeting, knowing that they wouldn't be challenged in front of an audience. It was quite funny when it happened, watching a face contort into a false smile as they listened to a gag they'd made a few hours before being played for laughs by someone who'd simply arch an eyebrow if confronted.

That was *never* what I was about. I wanted every show to be as good as it could be, and I saw my job as bringing out the best in the women. I was simply the conductor of the orchestra, encouraging them to make a beautiful sound. I gave up trying to explain, and every now and then began pushing back on an opinion or two in the meeting and getting a little feisty, just to keep everyone happy.

Being part of the show for so long meant I sat through many deeply emotional moments as well. The women bravely opened up on live television about terrible things that had happened to them or their families, because they knew that their vulnerability was what made our show so special; women at home felt they were watching real women like them, experiencing the same hardships and struggles. It was extremely powerful, and I felt very protective of us all, because I was also vulnerable with my own struggles during that time. During my years anchoring the show I experienced postnatal depression, relationship struggles, divorce, and surgically induced menopause, and I knew that talking about these experiences helped countless women who were experiencing the same things.

I felt that the panellists who contributed to these important conversations by sharing deeply personal stories about themselves needed to be offered support, not treated as simply fodder for the show, which was how it seemed to me.

During my time on *Loose Women* there was no counselling for any of us who shared intimate and painful stories with viewers. I asked for the programme to be provided with some kind of professional support, because every day we were being expected to poke our wounds, to reveal deep painful truths about ourselves and our experiences, with no aftercare. The after-show meeting was simply a case of, "That was great ladies, see you tomorrow where we will be talking about…" If your story appeared in the press, and they took what you said out of context, or you were trolled online, it all helped the ratings and the clickbait, so it felt like it was seen as great for the show. And that was it.

Getting support not only didn't happen, but I could also feel the attitude towards me from management change; apparently, I was no longer compliant, and that felt like it was a problem.

It was after participating in *SAS: Who Dares Wins* while anchoring *Loose Women*, that I realised how much support was needed on the show, especially as the experience caused difficult memories of extremely painful moments from my past to bubble to the surface. Regularly discussing personal pain publicly on *Loose Women* made the job uniquely challenging and highlighted a lack of adequate care.

Now, I completely understand that a personal experience of pain is not the responsibility of a workplace. Of course it isn't. I was paid to do a job, and I did it well, and in most circumstances that would be the end of it. However, it was an unusual job as it required discussing personal experiences of pain *in public*, which to my mind, changed the dynamic, and felt to me like a duty of care that wasn't met.

Though I can't detail my experience during my final 18 months at ITV for legal reasons, it was a tough period marked by a persistent culture where staff and freelancers were expected to "put up or shut up", to endure without complaint. The impetus to provide for my family and seeking therapy helped me cope, but eventually I chose to leave due to both personal struggles and ongoing insufficient support for women on the show.

I'm encouraged that friends say conditions have improved behind the scenes, but I'm sharing this now because I carried shame for my breakdown and departure, without being able to fully explain why. Instead, I went ahead and put all my effort into helping other women who felt stuck and scared – noble in theory but, as we now know, didn't quite succeed in practice.

I've been back on the show several times since, and returning was intimidating, but over time it became less so. Looking back, my exit was simply one moment among many in life – no big falling out, just a changed connection.

I remain proud of my role on *Loose Women*. It's one of British television's longest-running shows, and the only daytime talk show hosted solely by women. I love the viewers as much now as I did when I was there and would look into camera number one (the camera that was always on me as anchor) and wrap up a segment by making every woman watching at home feel like she was included in the discussion. It deserves every award it's ever got, and I am proud to have been a part of it. Though not every day was easy, I'm grateful for my experiences there and believe no one should feel ashamed for leaving a job when necessary.

# Lessons in Becoming Shame*less* in a Challenging Work Environment

1. **Can You Make This Work for You?**
   In the short term, finding a solution to a problem while staying in work is useful; a knee-jerk reaction is not, no matter what the problem is. Have your emotional reaction, which is justified and to be expected: cry, feel shocked or angry. Then think about what you can do about it. Is there a workaround? Can you offer a solution to a problem that you are on the short end of? All any workplace really wants is to have as few problems as possible and for everything and everyone to just "keep going", so is there a way to do that which serves you? This could mean teaming up with a colleague, brainstorming and offering up an alternative.

2. **Control What You Can Control**
   As the artist and burlesque performer Dita Von Teese famously said, "You can be a juicy ripe peach and there will still be someone who doesn't like peaches."[21] Not everyone is going to like you or support you, and you have to accept that. But if things are getting out of hand at work, keep a log of it. Dates, times, what was said, and who was present. If things blow over, then great. If not, and sadly you need to speak to your line manager or HR, you will at least now have a timeline to back up what you are saying. And – worst-case scenario – if you need to take legal action, you also have a record of action and response.

3. **Accept and Move On**

Some things simply can't be fixed, and the only solution is to move on. Try to reframe this as a positive thing while you are looking for another job. Sometimes just knowing that you are leaving is a boost to your confidence, even if no one else knows. You have value, you have transferrable skills, and you will find someone who needs what you have to offer. I'd urge you to have the confidence to control what you can control by deciding to move on. It's a big world out there, and sometimes we can get so involved in what is happening right in front of us and to us that we forget that.

If you have been affected by toxic work environments, I have included some links that offer advice and support in the resources for this chapter.

# 5

# LOVE HURTS, AND OTHER TRUTHS

*When It All Goes Wrong in Relationships,*
*and Everyone Has a Take on It*

> *"It's not my job to save people.*
> *It's not my job to fix people."*[22]
>
> Nedra Glover Tawab, *Mental Health Therapist and Author*

I am a sucker for a TikTok video.

I know you're not supposed to look at your phone before going to sleep, but I love to watch cute dogs do silly things. It helps me sleep knowing that somewhere out there, a dog is happily skateboarding or playing with a garden hose. I don't normally pay attention to other stuff on there, but one day something popped up on my feed that changed my perspective on love *forever*.

It was a video of a girl and her mother discussing the Disney film *Beauty and the Beast*. The mum was pointing out flaws in the story: that the Beast was very bad because he had captured Belle's father, and when she tried to rescue him, he imprisoned her instead. Plus, the fact that *the reason* he was a Beast was because he had been arrogant and unkind to an old woman, who was in fact an enchantress, so she cast a spell on him.

The Beast had previous.

The only way Belle could be set free was if she fell in love with him, despite him being vile to her. So, she is kind and patient and puts up with his miserable ways and even defends him when villagers come to rescue her. And eventually, yes, she falls in love with him because he's *a little bit nice to her*, and poof! Everything is right with the world.

Watching this TikTok video, the scales fell from my eyes.

How the hell had I not noticed before how awful this story is? How had I been so swept up by the cute teacup and catchy tunes while watching the film when my kids were young that I didn't spot the red flags? Surely imprisonment and gaslighting is right up there?

It struck me then that my own thoughts about romance, love, and acceptable behaviour had been moulded by this outdated idea: that a man was *supposed* to be moody and brooding, and would eventually soften and be nice to you if you waited around long enough, and were kind and patient, and didn't make a fuss about little things like gaslighting and cruelty (and perhaps the odd bit of imprisonment in a castle, but only if you were very unlucky).

## Constructing the fairy tale

I started reading my mum's old romance books when I was nine years old. We lived in The Philippines at the time, because my dad's job as an engineer meant moving around a lot and living in far-flung corners of the world. For over a year, we lived in a place so remote that there was no school and the electricity for the few buildings ran off a generator that was switched off every evening. The internet didn't exist back then, so all we had were the schoolbooks posted for my mum to work through with us, or the few comics we bought whenever we visited the nearest big town, a four-hour drive away on dirt track roads.

Any books I was bought on our infrequent trips to the capital Manila would be devoured in days, so I started borrowing my mum's Mills & Boon romance novels. I thought they were great and liked that the plots were the same: sweet, quiet wallflower intrigues the intense, handsome, rich guy, who leaves the sexy, experienced siren to sweep the quiet girl off her feet. The End. The books weren't saucy at all; they were tame compared to the stuff that kids see nowadays.

We also only had access to one television set, which was in the building where the expat men lived. There was no satellite TV so it couldn't show any actual telly, it could only play whichever videos we had. It is hard to imagine, but we lived miles from anywhere in a small circle of bungalows that housed expats brought in to help construct a brand-new sugar factory. There was one other couple, who were older than my parents and close to retirement, and another who kept to themselves, and a long single-storey building that housed the men who came to work on site without their families; it had basic bedrooms, a shared kitchen, and a TV room with one television and a VCR.

There were only two videos there that my younger sister and I could watch: *Star Wars* and *The Sound of Music*. That was all we watched for a *year*. I became very, *very* familiar with *The Sound of Music*. So much so that a few years ago it was my specialist subject when I appeared on the TV show *Celebrity Mastermind* – I came second to someone who really knew his Marvel movies. Gutted.

The narrative that I saw repeatedly played out in the film was the same: keep quiet, acquiesce, be good, and support your man. I even saw this in my mum and dad's relationship, which from the outside appeared to reflect this ideal. I'm now in my 50s and have a much more open and adult relationship with my parents, and I realise that what I thought I was seeing wasn't the case at all. My mum is a super-strong woman, whose quietness hides a steely core. She has very much been an equal partner to my dad – I just couldn't see it as a child.

This attitude explains a lot about my own relationships, and why I accepted the bad things I did for so long in the past – I literally didn't know any better. Perhaps, come to think of it, the men in my life didn't know any better either. Were they also raised in a world where this was how boys behaved? We are all affected by our parents' behaviour (something I will explore more in Chapter 8) and either subconsciously repeat or consciously rebel against it, so is it possible that every partner I chose was only doing their own version of what I was doing?

Perhaps it explained the response of one of my parents' friends, who, when he was introduced to me as "You know, the one off the telly who just got divorced again", replied, "Oh that's *you?!* The one your father keeps giving away, and you keep coming back!" That wasn't all. He continued, "Divorced *twice,* eh? In my day we had sticking power, didn't just give up when it all got too much. I've been with my wife for 52 years!"

I had a quiet word with my dad after that and told him that his joke about giving me away and me coming back wasn't *quite* as funny to me as it was to him.

One of the positives of having *two* failed marriages is that our family has had to deal with issues that many wouldn't, like having a blended family, and in my case two children from two different fathers. This throws up all manner of complications, and, when they were younger, took military precision to organise weekends, school holidays, and Christmases – never mind adapting to the sliding-scale attitude to parenting styles.

How are these things a positive?

Because I ended up being educated about the complicated ways of the world in a manner I never would have foreseen otherwise.

I thought I'd meet someone, fall in love, get married, and live happily ever after. And that would be it.

It seems very old fashioned now, but it was all I knew; my parents met at 15 and 16 and they are now in their 80s and happily together. They still find each other funny, which I think is half the battle.

My first love was a brooding teenager who I met at school. It lasted 17 years and produced my lovely son.

I thought I'd meet someone, fall in love, get married, and live happily ever after. And that would be it

My second relationship floundered because I had learned nothing at all from the first. With the benefit of hindsight, I can see very clearly that I was extremely naive. Friends and colleagues pointed out concerns, but – much like Belle in *Beauty and the Beast*, and every romantic novel I'd devoured – I thought the love of a good woman like me would make it all fine. I can honestly say I gave it my best shot for eight years, before accepting it was best to call time.

It was most definitely *not* fine and meant I lived through experiences that I am still emotionally processing to this day.

After seeing the TikTok video that blew open my understanding of the lies around romance I had been fed as a child, I decided to do some digging, and in the name of research asked my then-18-year-old daughter about attitudes to love and romance, to see how things have changed since I was a teen. What I discovered was astounding to me.

Wow.

It's a different world out there now.

She explained that the kind of thing she and her friends regularly watch are other girls sharing stories about their life on TikTok, normally while doing their makeup. Girls talk about how their boyfriends behave, and impart advice to their followers, all eagerly lapped up by people who don't have the life experience to challenge what they are hearing.

As one small example, some girls repeatedly moan about their boyfriends and tell their followers to break up with theirs if he doesn't buy them flowers or treat them like a princess at *all times*. I mean, on the plus side, it's great that they are setting a bar for themselves that is *way* higher than anything I did, but on the other, it all seems a bit, well, unrealistic?

The truth is that love hurts sometimes. In real life, we get things wrong, we make mistakes. And there is a huge difference between unknowingly being selfish or thoughtless, and deliberately and wilfully being abusive. But somehow these all get intertwined in the echo chamber of online chatter, which is repeated and replayed in real life. All this leads to one place… shame.

The shame of "getting it wrong" if your actions are deemed out of line. The shame of "getting it wrong" if you have accepted behaviour that is seen as out of line. Shame cast by people who have no idea what your life is really like.

This used to come from people you knew, perhaps at school or at work. But we now have instant online access to the lives of people we will never meet yet strangely have very strong opinions on and feel we have the right to freely express them.

## The double standards of romantic shame

This is something that is particularly true when it comes to women, who are expected to always behave in a way that is acceptable to… *other women*. The double standards of what behaviour is seen as perfectly fine when carried out by men, but not so by women, in our so-called "enlightened" times are shocking. What's happening in the world is often reflected and eagerly dissected through the experiences of (mainly female) celebrities. So many women have faced public shaming because of their relationships – whether for dating someone controversial, moving on "too fast" or "not fast enough" after a breakup, or simply for breaking the mould of what society expects from women in love.

Jennifer Aniston spent *years* being pitied or shamed for being "unlucky in love", following her divorce from fellow actor Brad Pitt. The constant narrative was that she was somehow too career-focused, too needy, or just not enough to keep a partner. Despite being hugely successful and talented, surrounded by loving friends and family, the "poor Jen just can't keep a guy" theme carried on for years, even after she spoke out about how deeply unfair, untrue, and invasive this scrutiny of her life has been.[23]

Taylor Swift, the global superstar, multi-award winner and whip smart businesswoman, just couldn't do right when it came to her relationship status, according to the press. Before her 2025 engagement to NFL player Travis Kelce, she was constantly slut-shamed and mocked for dating high-profile men and writing songs about her ex-boyfriends. Even though pretty much every male musician does the same thing, she faced *far* more scrutiny and public shame. She sells out stadiums around the world, something any aspiring musician can only dream of, male or female, yet is often reduced to just being a woman who moaned about her exes.[24]

No nuance, no grey area, and definitely no allowances made for information that you or I have no access to, which is essentially "what really happens in their lives". It simply doesn't matter how great they are at their job, how many awards they win, how kind they are to their fans, or how many employees they pay fairly and generously award bonuses to.

*"Yeah, she's not all that though."*

How do men of similar standing fare in the same kind of situations?

The first person who springs to mind is Mick Jagger. He's the same age as my dad, and throughout my adult life has been portrayed in the press as a lovable old rogue, the star who has had multiple affairs and fathered eight children with five different women, who remains a rock legend still performing to packed stadiums. Because he's, you know, *Mick Jagger.*

The actor Ben Affleck had a high-profile split from his then wife, actress Jennifer Garner. He then rekindled his previous romance with Jennifer Lopez and had a huge showbiz wedding, only to divorce a few years later. He is still a respected actor and director, albeit mocked for looking grumpy when he's snapped by the paparazzi – but fair enough, I'd look grumpy too if strange men leapt out from behind bushes to take pictures of me. It is Jennifer Lopez who is shamed in the press for being married a few times, for being too selfish and demanding, otherwise she'd have "kept her men".

The double standards would be jaw dropping if we weren't so used to them.

So why are men forgiven for their relationship choices, mistakes, or misdemeanours while women are not? Why does the public shaming continue for one and not the other? It's the same as in *Beauty and the Beast*: it's on the woman to be enough for the guy – only now it's not just the Beast she has to impress: it's the whole world.

## The pain of love gone wrong

We had a family conversation around the dinner table one night, which somehow ended up being about my relationship with my exes. I don't regularly speak to the fathers of my children, and a young adult guest at the table asked why this was. They thought it was odd that we weren't "raising our kids together". I explained that I had spent years in regular contact with them, to ensure that there was a continuity of care in terms of love, support, bedtime and TV rules, homework being done, birthday and Christmas celebrations – all the minutiae that comes with bringing up children in a divorced household.

My children are now young adults and can make their own arrangements to spend time with their dads. They chat on the phone, they FaceTime, they go on holidays – I'm not needed for this part. If there is a problem, or a celebration, and there needs to be a united front, then I am there, but otherwise, I don't have any need to be in their lives and they have no need to be in mine. We aren't together anymore, and we have our own lives to lead.

Our young guest found this odd. Surely we should be meeting for catch ups and chats? What will happen when there is a wedding, they asked, how will we handle it then? The table erupted into a chorus of "Oh my God! That's so stressful!" We are a blended family, so there were equal eruptions from both sides about who was going to walk whom down the aisle, who could come, and who would make whom feel uncomfortable. There was laughter as they chatted and tidied away the dishes.

But I didn't find it funny. I slipped out and cried in my bedroom, like Emma Thompson in *Love Actually* (albeit without the cheating husband), before coming downstairs and carrying on. I can only think that their youth and inexperience in the pain of love gone wrong means they can't fully understand that life just isn't that simple.

Sometimes you can't carry on as friends after a relationship breaks down. I can't speak for all cases, but in mine, the tears came because I felt that the inference was it's on me to keep smiling and keep being okay with things, because when it comes to some exes, you know, shoulder shrug, *that's just how they are.*

I accept that and, like many, have found a way to make it work. But there are exceptions to this. Sometimes the shame and pain that a person inflicts on another is so incomprehensibly huge that, justifiably, there is no coming back. My experience of relationship breakdown taught me how easily pain can be minimised and normalised. That understanding also shaped how I see domestic abuse more broadly – through listening to survivors, reading their accounts and recognising common patterns.

Domestic abuse is a hideous term. It underplays the psychological damage that it causes: the experiences that pierce like fishhooks and embed deep into your psyche, and which are as painful to wrench out as they were when they were inflicted. They leave a wound that no one can see.

If I can explain it in layman's terms, the wound is a fear inside your being, and a fear inside your own home, the place that is supposed to be your sacred, safe space.

It is natural to feel afraid if, when walking down a dark street, we hear heavy footsteps behind. But once we are behind our front door, and it is locked and the curtains are closed, this is where we are supposed to breathe out. Our shoulders are meant to come down, and our fight-or-flight reflexes lessen. We can slip into our comfy clothes, put on the TV, and relax.

For those living in an abusive relationship, that fight, flight, freeze, or fawn kicks in *when they get home*. They can tell in an instant what kind of evening they are going to have, and which of the responses they are going to have to implement to get through the night with as little fallout as possible.

Maybe they'll fawn; they'll ask about their day, listen and empathise and soothe, while doing all the things they know will keep them calm. Many survivors describe moments like these: make them a lovely dinner, listen to their escalating rant, agree that all of it is your fault, endure sex that feels violating rather than loving, and hope they fall asleep quickly. Soothe, smooth, hold your breath, and pretend it's all okay. Creep out of bed and cry in the shower and lay out your clothes for work the next day. Say nothing to anyone.

Maybe you'll freeze and do nothing, hoping it will blow over quickly and the kids won't hear.

Maybe they'll fight, but if they do, they know it will need to be followed by flight, and where will they go? The kids are in bed. There is school the next day, and work, and how will they explain it to them?

The fear response can be similar to that caused by an assault by a stranger. If someone followed you down an alleyway, and inflicted harm on you, no one would expect you to smile and sit next to them at a wedding. That would seem crazy, right? People would be supportive, and usher you away, reassure you that you are loved and safe, and never put you in such an uncomfortable position. They would understand that even though you're not in that alleyway anymore, just seeing that person and being in their vicinity is enough to make you feel sick and afraid.

Putting the word "domestic" in front of any kind of abuse has come to symbolise that it's simply a disagreement or misunderstanding that happens between couples in their home.

It happens. Don't make such a big deal. Whether it is physical, sexual, emotional, psychological, or narcissistic, any kind of pain deliberately, wilfully, and repeatedly inflicted on another person is abuse. The narrative around domestic abuse, whether it is inflicted on women by men, or on men by women, or in same-sex relationships, is pretty much the same. It's viewed as not being as bad as "proper" abuse. It can't be, because why would you put up with it? Why would you stay?

The answer is simple. Shame.

You "got it wrong". You ignored the warnings from friends that something wasn't quite right. You didn't see the red flags through the love bombing. You have become isolated from your family, and don't have anyone to turn to. You have a good job, and a reputation in your community. Maybe you excitedly posted pictures and updates about your wedding and honeymoon all over your social media and now have to shamefully explain that it's all over. Maybe you have been married before, and people will label you as flaky. So, you keep it to yourself, because if you do speak out, you'll be branded hysterical and need to get a grip. He's a great guy, and so good with the kids?

Yeah, it can't be that bad.

Sadly, it can, and often it is shame that keeps us in situations that are not just painful, but unsafe.

My advice to anyone feeling like this is to ask for help. I have listed some websites which provide advice and support for people who find themselves in any of these situations at the end of the book.

I can't talk about shame, and relationships, without mentioning one of the worst cases ever to shake our perception of domestic abuse. It revealed just how extreme the betrayal of marital trust could be, and how exploited and violated a woman could be within what is meant to be a union rooted in love and respect. It was a horrific case that rocked the world in 2024, when 72-year-old Gisèle Pelicot made the powerful decision not to remain anonymous but have a public trial after her discovery that her husband had, over nine years, repeatedly drugged her and invited strangers into their home to rape her.[25]

She refused to be shamed for something that she was a victim of, declaring, "Shame must change sides." By bringing her case into the public eye, Gisèle did something monumental. She transferred shame from the victim to the perpetrator, forcing them to be accountable for their actions rather than the other way around. How different the world would be if we could grasp that shame doesn't belong to us, and we could see that it is so often an unwelcome, unwanted, and underserving gift that others thrust upon us and we are expected to dutifully accept.

Her bravery transcended boundaries, and she was recognised as a global figure of triumph, strength, and dignity over shame, and hopefully will continue to pave the way for not only legal reforms but also societal change.

Because sometimes the Beast is hidden inside relationships that look safe from the outside.

That's the quandary that comes with forming a relationship with anyone; you just don't know what is going to reveal itself. But does that mean that we are better off without love, because it can bring us such gargantuan amounts of hurt and pain?

Absolutely not.

Love may hurt, but it also heals and rebuilds. I believe that it is the most powerful of all our emotions – more powerful than fear, and infinitely more powerful than hate.

In fact, I see hate as the shadow side of love; it's the reason why we so often end up hating those we used to love more than anyone else on the planet. If you feel indifferent about someone, they aren't going to spark a rigorous emotion from you. Whereas someone to whom you have given your tender, precious heart and trusted them to take care of it, only for them to smash it to pieces... well, you are going to have a bundle of emotions when it comes to them: hurt, anger, disbelief, grief, and shame that you "got it

Love may hurt,
but it also heals
and rebuilds. I
believe that it is the
most powerful of all
our emotions – more
powerful than fear,
and infinitely more
powerful than hate

wrong". Maybe you did, and maybe you didn't. Maybe you were vulnerable, or gullible, ignored the warning signs, or just saw what you wanted to see.

As the poet Alfred, Lord Tennyson famously wrote, "'Tis better to have loved and lost than never to have loved at all."[26]

It just doesn't always feel that way.

Do I regret the choices that I have made in my life regarding those I've given my heart to? Yes, but also, no. Some of my biggest heartaches have also led to my greatest learning, which I've been able to pass on to my children and to everyone who has read my books or heard me speak.

I have now been with my third husband for over a decade, and we have had to deal with some extremely challenging times together as a couple. I can't definitively say that I have my "Happily Ever After", because I now see that this is an impossible thing to know for sure. Ever After is far away, it feels like something to be aiming for, rather than something to be lived every day and in our own weird and idiosyncratic way. Are we happy? Yes. We love each other, we like each other, and we champion and cheer for the other. He is the first person I want to call when something happens, whether good or bad. He's my best friend, and I'm his, and I'm as proud of him as he is of me. We fancy each other and enjoy each other's company. We make each other laugh and we also annoy the hell out of each other. We can be completely ourselves, which sometimes means we show our ugly sides and are snappy, snippy, patronising, and thoughtless.

But we are always sorry, and there is always love. Always love.

# Lessons in Becoming Shame*less* in Love

1. **Treat 'Em Mean, Keep 'Em Keen Is a Lie**

   Yup, even though it appears in most romantic narratives, if it's love that you are searching for then it's simply not true. If you want excitement, drama, and quite a lot of trauma then yes, there it all is. Fill your boots if that's what you're after, because you will get it by the bucketload. There is a time in our lives when some types of drama can seem like fun, and it certainly makes for interesting conversation with our friends, but in the long run, if someone is getting off on making you feel ashamed about who or what you are, how you look, how you behave, and what they allow you to do or not do, then they are not the qualities to look for in a partner. Take my advice, excuse yourself and *run*.

   They do not need you to fix them or love them better, even if they are very sorry every time they mess you about. There is a simple saying, often attributed to the indomitable author Maya Angelou, that I encourage the young women in my family to remember when someone is behaving this way and causing them pain: "If someone shows you who they are, believe them." It's one to live by.

2. **It's Never Too Late to Start Again**

   Not everything is meant to last forever, and there may come a time when the most sensible thing to do, even though it is tough and painful, is to walk away.

   Love hurts when it goes wrong, this is undeniable. It's awful and there is no pain like it. But when you are ready, and only you will know when this is, there comes a time to ask yourself the question, "Now what?" What can you do to salve your heart and rebuild your self-esteem? What friends can you reach out to? What hobbies can you try to distract yourself? There is always someone, and there is always something, if you look.

3. **Love Is All Around Us**

One of my favourite films is *Love Actually*; it's got everything – first love, secret love, awkward love, grief, betrayal, hurt, excitement, and resolution. All the messy bits that we get wrong, and the beautiful parts that we get right.

The opening scene is voiced over by the actor Hugh Grant and shows footage of the arrivals gate at Heathrow airport. People run into each other's arms, smiling, tearful, and joyful at their reunion, as he explains why this place (the arrivals gate) makes him feel hopeful about the state of the world, which so often feels like it is a gloomy place. But love is always there, we just don't notice it because we are distracted by awful things that are happening, which makes us feel like the world is only full of hate and greed. Of course, those things are also there, and they always will be, but, as Hugh says, "If you look for it, I've got a sneaky feeling you'll find that love actually is all around."[27]

Check out the opening scene on YouTube and hear the full power of the words. I defy you not to cry. When we feel like love is awful, and that we have been sold a lie, it's worth reminding ourselves that we haven't. Love *is* everywhere, we just don't see it sometimes because we are looking for the wrong thing, in the wrong place, and sometimes with the wrong people. But it is there. It is all around us.

# 6

# LET'S TALK ABOUT SEX, BABY

## The Shameful Stuff We Don't Admit

*"The most important thing you can do to have a great sex life is to welcome your sexuality as it is, right now – even if it's not what you wanted or expected it to be."*[28]

Emily Nagoski, Sex Educator and Author

Just as with our ideas about relationships, our ideas about our bodies and sex are influenced by what we see and hear growing up. And while the word "pudendum" wasn't bandied about when I was a teenager, discovering that this collective name for the genitals is actually a medical term from a Latin word that means "to be ashamed", it's not surprising that every generation feels shame when it comes to our sexy bits. I mean, seriously? A part of our sexual anatomy is literally called something to be ashamed of, by doctors? *Come on.*

When I was growing up, I had a romanticised view of what sex would be like, based on the novels I read and movies I watched in the 80s. By the time I was 15, the sexiest thing I'd ever witnessed was the love scene in the film *Top Gun* between Tom Cruise and Kelly McGillis. It was all moody lighting with "Take My Breath Away" by Berlin playing in the background.

I was pretty late to the party in terms of sex, and I was okay with that. I never felt any peer pressure to lose my virginity, because to me, any friend who put pressure on me to do something I didn't want to do wasn't really a friend. I was very lucky to have that mindset, and to have great friends, so it was never an issue. There was no shame, or shaming, involved. I was in my first "proper" relationship for a year before I decided I was ready to take that huge step. I took myself to the doctors around my 19th birthday and started taking the pill. I waited until I knew it was safe, and then, it happened. I knew it would change everything between my boyfriend and me, and how I felt about myself, and I wanted to be sure I was okay about it. And I was. It was a good, healthy start to things, which I know I was very fortunate to have.

I'm also aware that my perception and experience of sex as a child and young woman is a world away from those of children, teens, and young adults navigating this today. It's ironic really; we all wanted more information about sex back then, because all we had to go on was what someone's older sister told us or the problem pages in teen magazines. It seems almost childish now, and while there are problems with not having easy access to vital information about sex, I think my generation had it easier than the teens and young adults of today, because we weren't overwhelmed with information and imagery that our not yet fully formed brains and emotions could cope with.

## From curiosity to overload

Kids and teens have always shamed each other when it comes to sex. It might be shame for what you know or don't know, for "doing it' or "not doing it", and everything in between. As adults we know this comes from a place of fear and insecurity, all wrapped in bravado, but we don't know that when we're kids.

Ironically, these days ready access to information about sex is part of the problem for teens, pre-teens, and young adults trying to work their way through the minefield of their burgeoning sexuality. The issue now is not a lack of information but being able to decipher what is true or helpful. It is now worryingly easy to access anything about sex, and to witness sex, online, even if you are not looking for it.

Teens would be incredulous now at the idea of walking into a newsagent, picking a pornographic magazine off the top shelf, and paying for it at the counter alongside someone buying fizzy pop or cigarettes. It took a lot more courage to access photos of naked people in the past than it does now, where you can accidentally stumble across something shocking while innocently looking for videos of happy dogs...

Sexual imagery has long played a part in sexual relationships. From instructional drawings in the *Kama Sutra* to titillating black and white photos of Victorian ladies wearing stockings and little else, we have always been curious and excited about what others do in bed. That's healthy, and helpful, and goes a long way towards eradicating the shame that is associated with nudity and sexual pleasure.

However, with the advent of the internet, and mobile devices allowing access to all things at all times, now pornography isn't simply naked pictures or videos of women or men having a grand old time. It can be graphic videos of violent sex that includes spitting, slapping, strangling, and extreme close-ups of anal, oral, and vaginal sex, with degrading, belittling "sex talk". The volume and scale of it is unprecedented, and it just keeps coming, with the algorithm offering up more and more of the stuff. Which could be hugely exciting at first, for anyone not now needing to buy something from a shopkeeper who might tell your mum or dad.

But what if you are being shown something you aren't emotionally mature enough to understand – or handle? Something upsetting, shocking, or confusing? Or if this is your introduction to sex? It's uncomfortable for parents at the best of times to talk about sex with their children, but if we ourselves hold shame around the subject and find it hard to discuss with our kids, then there is a strong possibility that our children will end up being educated about sex and sexual relationships purely through online content. Which, based on our outdated ideas as to what children are accessing, may not seem like a big deal. But it is.

A study carried out in 2023 by the Children's Commissioner for England, Dame Rachel de Souza, found that 80 per cent of teenage boys, and 50 per cent of teenage girls aged between 14 and 17 had seen porn online, and often had encountered sexual imagery before they had had any formal sex education.[29]

In the report Dame de Souza says:

"Let me be absolutely clear: online pornography is not equivalent to a 'top-shelf' magazine. The adult content which parents may have accessed in their youth could be considered 'quaint' in comparison to today's world of online pornography. Depictions of degradation, sexual coercion, aggression and exploitation are commonplace, and disproportionately targeted against teenage girls."

What does this mean? It means that things like rough sex and choking have become normalised, with shame playing a huge part in making girls and women compliant in acts that they don't always feel comfortable taking part in. Activities that were once considered niche are now in the mainstream, without context or nuance. And hey, I am not a prude, and I am most definitely happy for anybody to get their freak on, but where things get nasty for me is when it's uninvited, unreciprocated, and most definitely when it's obviously unwelcome.

On the plus side, some content creators are using their platforms to educate and share positive information for interested grownups as well as kids. For example, as well as being an entertaining content creator, Shan Boodram (@shanboodram on Instagram) is also registered with the American Association of Sexuality Educators, Counselors and Therapists. She uses her platform to interview famous people about their sex lives, providing informative content, and it's also really good.

## Becoming empowered

For women who enjoy erotica that is for *them* to get their rocks off rather than men, the adult filmmaker Erika Lust is a pioneer of ethical porn, which promotes a healthy depiction of sex, real communication, diverse bodies, and mutual enjoyment. Her creative team is primarily made up of female filmmakers, too, and judging from the behind-the-scenes footage shown on her Insta (which has already been removed from the platform twice for obvious reasons), the filming atmosphere appears to be relaxed, happy, and shame-free.

This is where shame around sex really seems to raise its ugly head. Because most shame stems from the idea of women *enjoying* being sexual. But here lies the paradox; enjoying sex is seen as shameful, but if a man leaves a relationship for sex elsewhere, this is also shameful, because you didn't keep him happy!

Pleasure is not a construct for servitude, where for women it can only be gained by giving pleasure to others, or allowing others to seek pleasure through you.

I remember being away on a work junket with a group of men and women I only loosely knew. A few of us had arrived at our location at the same time and were discussing what we'd do to kill time before our activities started, when one of the women matter-of-factly said, "I think I'll just unpack, have a wank, and join you later." It took every bit of muscle control to stop my eyebrows from shooting up my forehead. Especially when another woman in the group casually said, "Yeah, me too. See you later." This was a game-changer for me. *Why not* be casual about something that relaxes you, makes you feel less stressed and puts a spring in your step?

Despite *Loose Women*'s reputation for having feisty, strong women who weren't backwards in coming forwards, I remember a male guest being clearly (and foolishly, it turned out) desperate to tell a story about one of the panellists, an attractive single woman. A few years before, he had pulled up to a hotel at the

If you love each other, and sex has become something embarrassing and shameful, then it is *really* important that you talk about it same time as her and helped carry her bags into the foyer. As he did, something in one of the bags started vibrating strongly enough for him to feel it. He really milked this part of the tale; lots of winks to the studio audience and grinning from ear to ear.

We could all tell he'd dined out on this story for years and now couldn't wait to embarrass her on live television in front of millions. But he was messing with the wrong woman. She looked him straight in the eye and said, "Ah, yes, that's my electric toothbrush. I'm very careful about what I put in my mouth." We all burst out laughing, because we knew full well what she *really* always took with her in her suitcase. He was stumped. Shame: 0. Woman in charge of her sexuality: 1.

Being a woman in charge of her sexuality isn't something that I've ever given much thought to. It sounds like the kind of thing that belongs to bold women who are interviewed in glossy magazines and the big Sunday papers. I've read articles with women in midlife talking about how they reached their sexual peak in their 40s and 50s, and thought that sounded great, but it never had anything to do with *me*. Which explains why my first and only one-night stand in my 40s didn't quite work out the way I thought it would.

It began with a blind date that I didn't even want to go on. It was a few years after my second divorce and I didn't want to meet anyone, never mind start a new relationship. I was *done* as far as that was concerned. But, after much cajoling from a friend who told me not to overthink it, I went on a blind date. It was a double date with my friend and her husband, so less pressure. They were right, it was a lot of fun. I enjoyed my date's company, we had a spark, and I thought, why not? So, I asked to go home with him that night. I felt safe and I trusted him, so I instigated it, enjoyed it, and thought I'd never see him again.

We have been together ever since; because, yup, he became husband number three. Twelve years on, we have hung in there, and in that time life has thrown at us every imaginable obstacle and stress: mental and physical ill-health on both sides, surgical menopause following my hysterectomy (more about this in the next chapter), running a business together, the collapse of the business and the financial ruin that followed, plus raising a blended family and all the complicated ups and downs that come with that.

## Rediscovering desire

In middle age, and in marriage, one of the biggest casualties is sex. Often, from the female perspective (but not exclusively so), the mental load we carry means our heads are so filled with all the stressful things going on in our lives, and the things we need to do, that sex doesn't feature at all, because we are just *too tired*.

As a couple in our 50s, Nick and I have also experienced this. As I mentioned earlier, at one point I was recovering from Covid, dealing with prolonged stress and burnout, and was hospitalised with pneumonia, sepsis and kidney failure. It was *a lot,* so, as you'd expect, sex was the last thing on my mind. As I slowly got better, weeks, then a couple of months went by without intimacy. But it didn't go down well, if you'll excuse the pun. Normally I could gear myself up for it, and afterwards think, "That was actually nice, why don't we do that more often?" But not then.

I knew it wasn't just because my body was in pain and exhausted; my mind was also whirring with stress. My husband loved me very much, but he was becoming frustrated that I was emotionally, physically, and mentally flattened by the events of the past few years, and my illness was the last straw. In my eyes, he didn't "see" me – but he did, he just didn't like what he saw and heard, because I was constantly exhausted, stressed and ill, and was always talking about those things.

We argued about it during this time, when I asked him to do something and he (jokingly/not joking) said he would in exchange for sex. I got flustered and immediately felt anxious and under pressure not to reject or annoy him. I told him that for me sex starts in my mind, and I needed some wooing and to feel good, which would make me feel loving and attracted to him. He lost his temper, said that he was fed up with my negativity, and what the hell was all this about wooing? I didn't used to need wooing; I used to want it as much as he did! He became angry, defensive, and irritable. It was the worst reaction, because it made me retreat even further.

For two people who knew about this stuff, and were qualified to coach other people on it, it was interesting how all that knowledge falls apart when it is happening to you. We reverted to type.

Him: scared of rejection, lashing out and shutting down.

Me: scared of confrontation, retreating and shutting down.

Sex may have been the thing that brought us together on the first night of our relationship, but after everything we had gone through, would it be the thing that tore us apart?

Fortunately, we have the kind of relationship where we *are* able to talk things through, even ugly, awkward things. So yes, we found our way back to a place of understanding and love. Nick made an effort, and he bought a T-shirt off Amazon that says "I 'heart' my hot cougar wife", and when he puts it on, grins and winks at me; that's his version of wooing. It's not quite what I had in mind, but it makes me laugh, which is a good start.

I know that not everyone is so lucky. Menopause and andropause (the male version of the menopause) are a huge factor in depleting sexual appetite and activity for couples in their 50s and create a significant strain in the relationship. And it's hardly surprising to hear that shame plays a big part in this. Bodily shame, for starters: when your body doesn't look how it used to and will never "go back" it's enough to put you off. It takes robust self-esteem to think, "Sod it, this is who I am now, like it or lump it" and throw off your nightie with abandon. I know I wasn't feeling like that; I'd put on weight and felt exhausted, and most definitely not sexy.

I was experiencing sexy shame, which is not an official term, but you know what I mean. And it's a thing. In the peer-reviewed paper "Sexual Shame and Women's Sexual Functioning", shame on its own is described as: "...an attack on the self and at its core, holds the desire to be loved, valued, and seen as deserving and desirable."[30]

It is not surprising then that sexual shame ramps this up to another level. The same report describes *sexual shame* as:

"...a visceral feeling of disgust and self-abasement directed toward one's physical body, sexual being, and identity, and includes beliefs and feelings of inferiority, inadequacy, and helplessness, resulting in perceiving the self as flawed and defective."[31]

If shame is tied up in our need to feel safe, loved, and valued, and if our bodies and sexuality have previously played a big part in getting those positive feelings, then it makes sense that changes to our bodies and our mindset because of all the factors that life throws at us can leave us feeling inferior, defective, flawed, broken and – worst of all – unlovable.

This can happen at many times in our life, not just in midlife. Women are constantly changing, adapting, losing and gaining our sense of who we are, and of what makes us feel valued and desirable. Our sexual drive is not a constant, it waxes and wanes throughout all our junctions: puberty, motherhood, menopause, empty nest, and fluctuating health. I have had to start over many times because of these challenges, while the men in my life have carried on pretty much on a continuum, with no real understanding of how difficult the challenges are.

So, what can we do to get ourselves back in the saddle, as it were?

So many things spring to mind. All of them awkward and cringey. It's hardly surprising that most people would rather poke themselves in the eye than face the agony of being poked by anything else. The first thing to ascertain is whether the shame surrounding intimacy is physical or psychological. Is there a physical reason why things hurt, or won't rise to the occasion, or you don't feel enthusiastic about the idea of having sex? If so, then seeing a medical professional first is a good start. And it's less awkward, as it feels less sexual. Which means you're not making a fuss, which we Brits like.

Once the body has been checked out, it's time for the mind. This is where most problems lie when it comes to sex, even though we don't want to admit it. The first step is communication. Talk about it, even though it is uncomfortable and you're worried that it'll make things worse. If you love each other, and sex has become something embarrassing and shameful, then it is *really* important that you talk about it. Maybe bring up the idea of having an "Ugly Truth" or an "Embarrassing Truth" conversation and acknowledge that it's going to be awkward but at least you are communicating.

Here are some ideas, gleaned from my hard-won personal experience, on how and when to have a conversation with your partner when you feel sexually disconnected from one another:

- Do your research: this way it feels less like a personal attack. Understanding that it is normal to have sexual fluctuations in a relationship, and you are not alone, is key.
- Book in a time to talk: definitely don't talk about it while you are actually in bed. Do it when the kids are out and leave your phones in another room. Better still, go for a walk so that you are side by side – it doesn't feel quite so confrontational.
- Don't be combative: reassure them that the conversation is about finding your way back to having fun again. It's not about blaming and shaming, even if you really want to yell in frustration.
- Listen as much as you speak: even if what they are saying seems selfish or out of context, or just nonsense, let them say

it without interrupting. A good way to make sure you are both doing this is to repeat back what you have heard, as in, "So, what I'm hearing is…", which gives you both the chance to stay on track with having your say and making sure the message has been heard.

- Thank them for being honest and open: it is so important to acknowledge the vulnerability of what you have both just done – trusting that the person you are saying it to will respond with empathy and love.

Talking about sex is embarrassing and exposes you in a way that no other subject does. Well… maybe apart from talking about being in debt. Owning up to liking something, or not liking something, or feeling a certain way that may be at odds with how you behave or appear in every other part of your life is awkward, and the fear of being rejected is real. It's hideous. The potential for shame is at warp factor 10. But it's *so* important to do.

If ever there was a time to take a deep breath and make the first move (and yes, the other time is facing the truth about the hideous debt you're in and calling the people you owe money to), it's when intimacy has gone and you'd like it back again please.

# Lessons in Becoming Shame*less* About Sex

1. **Sex Is Nothing to Be Ashamed Of**

   How we feel about sex often stems from our introduction to it, or our caregiver's attitude towards it, but this doesn't have to affect the way we feel about it for the rest of our lives. As an adult, it's important to figure out how *we* feel about it, which stems from our own personal experience rather than what has been passed down to us.

   Sex is supposed to be pleasurable, and fun, so if it is neither of those things then it's time to check in with yourself. Ask yourself some simple questions: what do I feel when I think about sex? Is it something shameful? Is it something I must do to please others? Is it something I enjoy, or don't enjoy? Why is that? Is it a mental or physical thing? Where did I get my feelings about sex from? Do they fit with how *I* think I should feel? For example, if you feel guilty about the very idea of being sexual, or believe that it's dirty or slutty to find pleasure in it – where did these ideas come from, and do they serve you? We are all different, and you may have the same ideas as your caregivers, or you may have a different idea about it altogether. As long as it works for you, makes you feel good, and is legal and consensual, then crack on.

   In terms of figuring out what you enjoy experiencing sexually, it makes sense to work this out on your own, without the pressure of making sure that your partner is happy, so get used to the idea of self-pleasure as a way of making yourself feel good. How can you let a partner know what you like if you don't know it yourself? Plus, knowing that you don't have to rely on anyone else to provide you with sexual pleasure is a release in itself.

2. **Tell Me What You Want, What You Really, Really Want**
   Adding a little spice to things means being completely open
   about what you want. How many times have you moaned
   about never getting what you want – in life, love, or anything
   – when you have never actually asked for it? People aren't
   mind readers, and no matter how well you get along with a
   partner, they can't know what's going on inside your head
   unless you tell them. If you haven't been clear about what
   you want, and this goes for every part of your life, not just
   your sex life, you *cannot* moan that it hasn't been
   given to you.

3. **It Takes Two**
   Sex is something that both of you really need to be on the
   same page about. Agreeing that you'll do things simply
   because it brings pleasure to your partner, and they will do
   the same for you, can mean you are communicating and
   being loving and generous-minded. Anything that feels
   coerced, forced, or damaging in any way is *not* part of a
   healthy sexual relationship and needs to be discussed, either
   between you both or with a therapist.

   You will find details of experts who can help you work
   through any sexual problems you may be experiencing in the
   resources section at the back of this book.

# 7

# IS IT ME, OR IS IT HOT IN HERE?

*When Menopause Strikes*

*"My mind is like an internet browser. I have 19 tabs open, three of them are frozen, and I have no idea where the music is coming from."*

*Anonymous meme*

The atmosphere was hot and heavy, and not in a good way. Tension simmered as the car slowed and pulled over.

My dad turned to face my sister and me sitting in the back seat, as my mum glared out the window, teeth clenched, rage seeping from every pore. "Girrrls," he said, in his thick Scottish burr, "your mum is going through The Change. We are all going to have to be patient."

He turned around, put the car into gear, and off we went.

My mind was buzzing. The Change? It was the 1980s and *Teen Wolf*, the movie starring Michael J Fox, was in the cinemas. Oh my freaking God, was my mum a *werewolf*?!

That was how much I knew about the menopause as a teenager. Fast forward thirty-odd years, and my knowledge around The Change was still woefully limited.

### The stuck coil that saved me

I found out I was officially perimenopausal (where you still have periods but experience the symptoms of the menopause) by accident, when my contraceptive coil got stuck. If you are of a squeamish disposition, you may want to look away. I was about 43, and my GP, after lots of tugging and pulling, couldn't yank it out. She eventually admitted defeat against my incredibly strong vagina and sent me to a doctor who specialised in sexual, reproductive and menopausal health. What a twist of fate that turned out to be.

My new doctor removed my coil and gave me an internal examination to make sure everything was okay before inserting a new one. She casually asked, while rummaging around inside me, if I was experiencing any menopausal symptoms. I said I'd been having night sweats for a few years, and for a long time I'd been feeling "not quite myself". After a longer conversation about my lifetime of endometriosis, the rigidity of my vaginal walls (so it wasn't sheer strength after all), and the symptoms I was experiencing, plus the fact that my mother had gone through early menopause at 40, she wrote me a prescription for a transdermal oestrogen gel.

I was the luckiest woman in Britain. I was diagnosed as perimenopausal early thanks to my stuck coil and access to a brilliant NHS doctor. It was the luck of the draw. Not only did I have a doctor who was interested in and knowledgeable about the menopause, but she wanted to help and could.

I knew I was fortunate, but I didn't realise just *how* fortunate I was until, while writing this book, I investigated the menopause facilities available to women around the UK. The results weren't good. Even now, over a decade after my initial consultation, a shocking survey of 900 women carried out in 2025 by the blood test firm Medichecks shows that 93 per cent of women who had visited their doctor about their symptoms felt ignored, and had taken matters into their own hands to seek help elsewhere.[32] Official statistics indicate that over half a million women in the UK were waiting to see a gynaecologist in 2024.[33] Half a million!

GPs themselves acknowledge that the training they receive is not up to scratch. In a survey of NHS General Practitioners working across the UK, more than half said that they had not had enough training or support to be able to appropriately advise and treat women with menopausal symptoms. More than three quarters of GPs said they felt there is a need for better training in medical school.[34] Simply put, this means that if you are a woman and go to see your GP about physical or psychological symptoms in midlife that might be related to the menopause (which can affect women from age 35, by the way, so don't think this is just about us oldies), it is likely they won't know enough to be able to help you. Imagine if med school left out training about the liver because it didn't seem important?

What's interesting, and not in a good way, is that even those who work in women's sexual and reproductive health don't always join the dots when it comes to the kind of care that's needed.

A few years after my stuck coil incident, my endometriosis flared up again and the pain became unbearable. I had known that one of my options was to have a hysterectomy, but I hadn't previously wanted to do that because it felt drastic and would definitely mean no more children. But by the time I was 46, I knew I didn't want the pain or the children, and so on the advice of my doctors, I booked myself in. I underwent a full hysterectomy in 2016 and, because my endometriosis was everywhere, had everything removed: womb, ovaries, cervix – the lot.

I completely underestimated how big a deal this was, because naively, I was only thinking about removing the endometriosis. So too, it seemed, were the doctors. But removing parts of a woman's body that produce the hormones she needs to properly function mentally, physically, and emotionally, without making sure that these are replaced, makes no sense at all.

There was very little discussion about the need for HRT after my operation, because I'd said I was already on it and that seemed to be enough. I didn't realise that the dosage I was taking didn't factor in my entire hormone-producing engine being removed, and that my body would now no longer naturally make any oestrogen at all. So, I went into freefall.

Surgical menopause is unlike "normal" menopause, where things creep up on you. With surgical menopause, one moment you are kind of normal, and the next, it's like you are tipping over the edge of a very scary rollercoaster at full speed, screaming and disorientated, as your hormones plummet.

Again, I was incredibly fortunate to have access to a menopause specialist, who adjusted my HRT dosage. Despite making these changes just a few weeks after my operation, it took a long time for me to feel anything close to normal. I'd say with hindsight that it was a few years, but you don't realise it at the time because you just keep going. I felt "okay" and managed to continue with my personal and working life at the pace I had done before, without making a fuss, which is the default of so many women.

## How I became an accidental advocate

It is completely understandable that women feel shame discussing their menopausal symptoms with anyone, let alone people they work with. We grew up with it being shrouded in secrecy. We have fought long and hard to be treated equally and with respect, and many women have told me they felt that bringing up their mental and physical discomfort would set them back at work, or worse, could give their boss a reason to let them go. I was lucky that I worked in a predominantly female environment, where many of us were experiencing menopausal symptoms and discussing them, so there was no shame – at least not about the physical side of things. We all knew about popping a panty liner into the armpit of our blouse to stop sweat marks from showing on camera. But talking about it with work friends was very different to sharing tales of brain fog and exhaustion in public.

It was pointed out to me that I would have to give a reason why I'd be off the screens for six weeks while I recovered from my hysterectomy, in case the newspapers thought I'd been fired. So, the day before my operation, I unwillingly stuttered my way through a quick explanation on TV about what was happening.

Twenty-four hours later, while I was unconscious on an operating table, over 10,000 women contacted the show. Many began messaging me on social media, too, with a tsunami of questions about how I was going to deal with my menopausal symptoms after my hysterectomy, and what could I recommend to them? So many women told me about what they were experiencing, and the debilitating shame they were feeling about their symptoms: they couldn't cope with work or their family responsibilities; they felt overwhelmed, anxious, couldn't think straight, and their joints hurt; they were overheating and sweating at work, which was embarrassing and demoralising; their employers didn't understand, and they felt too ashamed to ask for support so were quietly trying to sort it out themselves. Could I help?

I had no idea that this moment would change everything for me.

It was an impossible task to reply to everyone, and I was also aware that I didn't know the answers to many of their questions. I decided to get as many answers as I could and put it all together in one helpful place: a book. I contacted my menopause expert, Dr Tina Peers, who agreed to write the medical side of things to back up my personal experience, and set out to create a first person-led, expert-backed book on the menopause.

This may have been something that women needed and wanted, but not everyone thought it was a good idea. My agent told me it was career suicide to associate myself with the menopause. I would be seen as old and past it, and I would lose work because of it as the word itself represented everything about being an "older woman". This came with its own challenges in day-to-day life, but for a woman in the workplace, and particularly in the media, where there is always someone younger and faster snapping at your heels, any association with ageing was a negative one. The resounding attitude to the menopause back in 2017 (and it is so nice to be able to say "back then") was that it was something that old women went through, which made them go a bit crazy. It was *not discussed* in public, and the only time it was brought up on television was when comedians dressed as old women and took the mickey out them.

But I was determined, and by 2018 the book was written and released.

And this was where the fun began.

My book *Confessions of a Menopausal Woman* was well received by the women who read it, and I'm still very proud of the fact that it was one of the first written by a woman in the public eye to offer a personal and medical insight into the menopause. I know it has helped thousands of women, and also men, to understand this time in a woman's life.

However. During press interviews I was asked how the public could help support women experiencing menopausal symptoms. I told how I was travelling on a train a few days previously when I saw a woman shedding her coat, then her jumper, then reach over and open the window even though it was freezing cold outside. There were mutterings from within the carriage, as people didn't understand that she was obviously experiencing a hot flush. The reporter asked what I'd suggest, and I replied, off the top of my head, that perhaps, just as we have badges that declare women are pregnant and need a seat, we could offer the same for women going through the menopause so people could understand that she was having a hot flush. The journalist laughed, and asked what the badge would say, would it be an "M" for Menopause? Maybe something like that, I replied.

It was off the cuff, and I didn't give it another thought. Until a few days later when I was in a meeting about some work outside of my TV job, and one of the women said they thought my "M" badge idea was pretty out there, and it was no wonder the press had gone so crazy about it.

It. Was. Everywhere. "Andrea McLean says menopausal women should wear M badges." Which is *not* what I said.

For context, *The Handmaid's Tale*, the brilliant drama starring Elisabeth Moss, was on television at the time. We were all talking about the dystopian society where women were publicly shamed into silence and servitude, with all their rights removed. The "M" badge controversy fit nicely in this narrative, and the media loved it. Newspapers did polls and ran headlines saying: "Menopausal Women Say No to M Badges!" Talk radio shows and TV panel shows got hours of airtime out of it, and people were *not happy.* The fact that it wasn't quite what I'd said, and definitely not what I'd meant, made no difference; it was whipped into a media storm, and I was at the centre of it.

How did that feel? Not great. I don't mind people disagreeing with me, but it was pretty awful having people getting angry with me for something that wasn't entirely true.

While it wasn't fun, I was genuinely glad that at last people were talking about the menopause. For the first time, it had become a hot topic of conversation. Men were talking about it, which was unheard of. They were discussing symptoms and the consequences of those symptoms. Even though it was misguided, and some might say deliberately misinterpreted, it had sparked debate, which I felt was a good thing. Did I jump in and keep the furore going? No. I did a single interview on morning talk-show *Lorraine,* where I knew it would be brought up in conversation, and put the record straight.

This is when I began building my This Girl Is On Fire blog, to help women in my own way, in all parts of their life. Just as I didn't want to be defined as "that menopause woman", I felt that surely women generally didn't want to be defined as that. We just wanted help and good advice and not to be penalised at work or in relationships because of our experience of the menopause, and for it not to be shameful or taboo.

I am obviously not the only high-profile woman to talk about her experiences and offer advice; the author and entrepreneur Meg Mathews, former wife of Oasis frontman Noel Gallagher, was a major forerunner in giving advice and promoting products designed to ease the symptoms of the menopause. She was also happy to discuss things that made people feel uneasy but were so necessary. I remember interviewing her the previous year on *Loose Women*, where she discussed the importance of masturbation in helping the vagina function properly. The UK collectively gasped: a woman openly admitted to masturbating! Had she no *shame?* Thankfully not, and she helped huge numbers of women to take control of not just their symptoms, but also their embarrassment. I thought she was fabulous.

Years later, it is interesting to reflect on that time, and the furore that was caused by the idea of women discussing masturbation, or of letting the world know through a simple message on her clothing that she was going through the menopause. This natural thing, that happens to 13 million women in the UK at any one time and will occur to half the world's population, is as normal a stage of life as puberty.

## The need for change

Time and time again, women have not sought help with menopause symptoms because of shame and embarrassment. In the workplace, the Fawcett Society report in 2022[35] revealed that 1 in 10 women had left a job because of their symptoms, and 77 per cent said there was no support available to them. Women working in predominantly male environments are understandably more likely to quit their job due to their menopausal symptoms because of shame. Being laughed at or dismissed because you are feeling anxious, experiencing brain fog and sleepless nights, is enough to

This natural thing, that happens to 13 million women in the UK at any one time and will occur to half the world's population, is as normal a stage of life as puberty make anyone walk away. The numbers "1 in 10" probably don't sound like much, so let's put them into context.

According to a 2023 report by the Office for National Statistics,[36] there are approximately 4.5 million women aged 45–60 in the UK workforce: the age group most likely to be affected by menopausal symptoms. If one in ten of them quit their job because they feel shame and embarrassment about this and aren't getting the support they need, that means around 450,000 women. Almost half a *million*. And this doesn't include those who reduce their hours, step back from leadership roles, or choose early retirement.

Changing public perception around the menopause has largely been credited to TV presenter Davina McCall's 2021 documentary *Sex, Myths and Menopause,* which tackled the misinformation surrounding HRT and the shame that many women felt about their experiences. It was definitely a pivotal moment, where the gathering momentum towards open discussion saw the tipping point into the menopause being something that could be talked about openly, without ridicule and shame.

Things are thankfully changing, thanks to the hard work and dedication of women like women's health ambassador Dame Lesley Regan, MP Carolyn Harris – who introduced the Menopause Bill to Parliament in 2021, which led to reduced HRT costs and improved access to support[37] – and Mariella Frostrup, the journalist, broadcaster, and founder of Menopause Mandate, which has helped to raise media attention around the need for policy change in the workplace. Mariella and her counterparts played a huge role in changes made to NHS guidelines in October 2025, which *finally* saw menopause questions and support introduced as part of general health checks in England.[38] This, alongside the governmental appointment of an independent Menopause Employment Champion,[39] encouraging employers to develop supportive menopause practices at work, will hopefully see changes implemented sooner rather than later.

There is still a long way to go to remove generational shame and stigma around the menopause, and making changes to current and future healthcare provision and working practices is a good start. But what makes the most sense is removing shame at the source, and that starts with educating the next generation. This is finally happening thanks to the work of Diane Danzebrink, the founder of campaign group Menopause Support, which has helped bring about the inclusion of menopause into the Relationship and Sex Education curriculum in England.[40] My daughter has at least heard of it, because we talk about it openly in our home, but I know not all homes are like that.

Women are horrified when we hear about teenage girls who are not informed about the changes that happen to their bodies when they go through puberty, and who are shocked and frightened by blood in their underwear because they have not been told what a period is. We understand that removing fear, shame, and embarrassment so that this natural transition from girlhood into young adulthood is as easy as it can be is the right thing to do. But it wasn't always so, and generations of girls grew up not knowing what was happening to their changing bodies. One day, I am hopeful that we will look back at the time when women were ill-informed and shamed into dealing with the challenges that come with the menopause on their own, with no support, and shake our heads in disbelief.

The next stage, alongside educating girls, is educating boys and men about the menopause. Something I saw many times when I was running This Girl Is On Fire was, as women became more knowledgeable and less ashamed, they felt more able to talk to their partners and husbands about what they were experiencing so that they understood. My husband Nick had a steep learning curve when it came to understanding the challenges women face and how best to support them. He now coaches both men and women going through challenges in their work and personal life and tells me that one of the biggest obstacles is men not knowing anything at all about why their wife might potentially "change" in midlife.

It's obvious if you think about it, because while there has been a lot of noise regarding the menopause, it has been made by women to help women, so men have tuned out: they feel this doesn't concern them, it's a "women's issue".

This came into sharp focus recently when I hosted an event about midlife, and there was only one man, Philip Baum, in the audience. He was there to support his cousin, who was the woman I was interviewing, otherwise he'd never have come. Having been introduced before the event and instinctively knowing that he wouldn't take offence to the question, I asked him in front of the crowd how he felt about being the only man in the room. His response was wonderful. He said that he wasn't surprised to be the only man there but was so glad he had come because he hadn't realised how blinkered he had been, and he realised that all the men he worked alongside are the same. He said that he was going to do something about it the very next day, and he did. For context, Philip is an aviation security expert, and the Visiting Professor of Aviation Security at Coventry University.

This is his post about the event on LinkedIn, which he has kindly allowed me to share with you:

"Chairing the discussion with Katie [Taylor] was Andrea McLean, who asked me how I felt, as the only man present, listening to the issues being raised. My response – embarrassed. Not embarrassed, however, about the subject matter. Rather that it, like pre-menstrual tension, should, in an era when we talk more openly about mental health issues, still be considered a somewhat taboo topic for men to engage with. Surely all men – especially those in the workplace – should have an appreciation of the challenges women may well experience in midlife?

For example, I've sat through countless presentations explaining causal factors for unruly passengers: intoxication, claustrophobia, fear of flying are all cited as influencing (not justifying) disruptive behaviour. I don't think anyone has ever mentioned women's health issues. If a passenger – or fellow crewmember – were experiencing hot flushes, fatigue, lack of energy, anxiety, low mood, headaches, heart palpitations and/or pain (just a few of the symptoms of menopause), might that not explain (again, not justify) a passenger reacting inappropriately ...especially whilst being propelled through the air in an aluminium tube at 33,000 feet after a night of no sleep?

Meanwhile, in any industry (and especially in aviation), our female workforce could be at the peak of their careers aged 40–55 and employers are at risk of losing valuable talent if appropriate support is not offered and the challenges of menopause (and perimenopause) are not better appreciated.

Suffice to say, it's a topic worth adding to the curriculum – as I did this morning on my course on behaviour detection. An exclusively male class of security officers in Dublin agreed it was refreshing to discuss and, reassuringly, they did so without a single snigger."[41]

I was thrilled at Philip's response. As an aviator, it was one small step for him as a man, but a giant leap for mankind.

All change begins with one tiny step. They are barely noticeable at first, and seem to make no difference, but bit by bit we get closer to making the change we want and need. Our involvement in any kind of change can happen by accident: having to tell the world about my hysterectomy led to writing a book, which led to creating a business, which led to me leaving my TV career, which ultimately led to me writing *this* book on challenging our ideas about shame. Or change can happen by chance: one man coming along to an event to support his cousin has led to changes in aviation security training. Or it can happen by choice – sometimes we simply feel a need to get involved and shake things up until they change for the better. It doesn't matter why, or how – what matters is that if we are able, we do.

# Lessons in Becoming Shame*less* in Menopause

1. **The Change Is Coming...**
   The menopause is a stage of life all women go through, whether we like it or not, so we may as well find out as much as we can, figure out what works for us, and learn to ride the waves. I am happy with the change in attitude that has happened in my lifetime when it comes to talking about the menopause, and the incredible amount of help and support that is now available. A brilliant book that is such a help for all women in midlife is *Midlife Matters* by Katie Taylor – and yes, it was her book event that I was hosting, where there was one man in the audience.

2. **Talk to Men About It**
   It's one thing having an impassioned and informed conversation about something in a place where everyone is going through the same experience and understands. But to get any kind of meaningful support, these conversations need to happen with people who can help effect change. That means men. Encourage them to read books like the one above or watch any programmes that you have found helpful. Talk about your experiences and ask how they can share what they know with their friends in a helpful way. The more

they know, the more they will understand and the better your relationship and eventually your workplace will be. It's win/win.

3. **Get Help**

   You don't have to grit your teeth and get through this alone. Keep a list of all your symptoms and develop an understanding of their regularity and intensity. Then go and see your doctor, and if they aren't helpful, visit a menopause specialist. You wouldn't "put up with" a broken leg or toothache, so don't feel you have to with the menopause.

8

# BREAKING THE CHAIN OF GENERATIONAL SHAME

*If It All Starts Here, Are My Kids Ruined?*

*"They fuck you up, your mum and dad.*
*They may not mean to, but they do.*
*They fill you with the faults they had*
*And add some extra, just for you."* [42]

*Philip Larkin, Author and Poet*

The chair was hard and wooden, and dug into my knees as I knelt on it. I pulled myself up to standing, feeling the chair wobble a little under my feet. No one was looking. They were talking, deep in conversation, and cooing over the moses basket containing my brand-new sister. I pulled my dress up to my head and stuck out my rounded three-year-old belly, wiggling from side to side. "Look at me!" I shouted. "Look at me!"

Horror on faces. Being plucked into the air and tucked under an arm and taken to what was now "our" bedroom by my dad. My mum, red faced and angry, hissing at me: "Stop this right now! You've had your turn!"

This is one of my earliest memories of shame. Of my parents being angry with me because I had embarrassed them, and the feeling that "my turn" of being loved by them was over, because another, newer child was now here.

I had long forgotten about that moment, but it came to mind 50 years later when I was being led through timeline therapy, where you are taken back through moments in your life that have formed thoughts and feelings around certain situations, allowing you to look at them through informed, adult eyes. I saw myself clearly, standing on that chair, and felt the hot shame of being admonished. The therapist asked how I felt looking at it as an adult, and how I felt about my parents reacting in this way. I experienced a surge of love and compassion for them, seeing them as a young, exhausted couple with friends and neighbours that they wanted to impress. I saw that they did the best they could with the tools they were given as parents, and that they were just starting out, and figuring it all out, just as I did with my children and as my children will with theirs.

Years later, in a coaching session with a client, we were discussing the effect of sibling order within the family. I am an older sister and have always behaved like an older sister. By that I mean well-behaved, wanting to please, helpful, hardworking, sensitive, and takes criticism very personally through fear of rejection. Yup, I tick *all* the boxes.

My client then told me about research she was doing on the impact of birth order and how it is reflected in how you parent your own children. She asked about my mother, who is the eldest of two with a younger brother. She explained that there will have been a moment in my mother's young life when she was everything, and then she was second best. She lost in rank to her younger brother, because even though she was the eldest, she was a girl. Her younger brother would have outranked her, and she was now inferior to him in her parents' eyes. She'd had her turn, and now it was over. Clearly this is a theory, and I have no idea if this is how my grandparents actually felt about my mum and her brother, but it was a shocking thing to hear.

Once again, I felt a surge of love and compassion for my mother. They say you only truly appreciate your parents when you become a parent yourself, but that is only partly true. You carry on learning to understand your parents more with every passing year, as life throws up challenges that you handle as best you can but don't always get right. Just as they did, and their parents before them. My parents are now in their 80s, and I love and appreciate them more than ever and am grateful that they were the parents I was gifted with.

As children, we think that our parents know what they are doing, that they have it all figured out, and it is only when we become grownups ourselves that we realise none of this is true. Which is terrifying – who is in charge?! Oh my God, we are! And we are making it up as we go along.

I remember the day I came out of hospital with my firstborn, my baby son. It was day three, the Baby Blues day when hormones flood your poor body and everything feels overwhelming. We had driven home at a snail's pace and gently placed the car seat with this tiny baby inside onto the living room floor. He looked so small, so defenceless, and the overwhelm was huge. I began to cry. How could the hospital *possibly* have let us leave with this baby? We didn't know how to look after him! My husband at the time told me to go upstairs and sleep, and that we would be fine. I did, and somehow it was. In the world of parenting, you figure out what problem you are going to solve that day and count your blessings if you manage to do it. That day, we did.

## Learning to be ashamed

As I've touched on in the first chapter of this book, shame is the feeling that we are flawed, wrong, or bad in some way. Guilt is the feeling of *doing* something bad, while shame is the feeling of *being* something bad. When we understand it this way, it's easy to see how these internalised feelings begin when our ideas about our identity are being formed. This relates to Charles Horton Cooley's concept of the "looking-glass self" that I discussed in Chapter 3; this idea that our concept of who we are is based on what *we think* other people think we are. And those "other people", when we are just starting out in life, are our caregivers. As children, we don't internalise feelings of shame or not being good enough because of something we do, but because of others' reactions to us. Shame is something we learn.

Think of a child who does something silly and everyone laughs and claps. You can clearly see how much they enjoy the reaction of love and laughter and will keep doing the silly thing to get the same response. Now take that same child, and the same silly thing, and put them in a room with parents or adults who scold them for being stupid. Their understanding of who they are will be influenced by this reaction; they did a silly thing and have been told they are stupid, therefore they *are* stupid. They have become a living, breathing definition of shame. It's heartbreakingly simple.

While we know in theory that our childhood experiences influence the adults we become, how can you spot this? Think about your own friendship groups, or relationships, and whether what you witness and experience is "toxic", an overused word of our time, or whether it is due to childhood shame.

Consider the woman who was fed by her narcissistic father's love but still fears his rejection and so measures her worth in being better or smarter or more successful than others, yet never feels good enough, and is envious of and despises anyone who outshines her. The man who grew up in an abusive home and saw conflict and violence as the norm and repeats the behaviour in his own relationships. The woman who was rejected as a baby, raised in a poor, chaotic home, and imagines the way to gain love and keep it is through material worth, and shuts down in conflict because she fears being rejected again.

There are hundreds more examples of behaviour that is exhibited as an adult who should know better but is steered by the child within. Yet it doesn't have to stay this way. Once we know better, we can do better, and uncovering the shameful parts of ourselves, the ideas of who we are that were formed before we knew how to rationalise them, is the first step towards this. And it all starts with the story we have been told about ourselves, and the story we tell *ourselves* about ourselves.

This is something that we aren't even aware of; I certainly wasn't aware that I was telling myself a story and living by it until I was well into adulthood. Luckily for me, most of my story was good, because I had parents who encouraged me to be brave, to try hard, to get back up after a setback, and believe that I was capable of achieving my dreams. But subliminally, the story was also firmly embedded that I had to seek approval for everything I did from the people I loved, and when engaging with the wrong people, this meant squashing down the parts of me that made the parts of them feel inferior.

It's so interesting once you can step to the side and observe this behaviour in yourself. We all do it; we are all simply adult children, still responding and behaving in ways that we were trained to. It's usually not until something drastic happens that sends us to a therapist or a life coach that we can better understand them, having been gently shown what we are doing and given the tools to detach and observe our actions and reactions, and those of others.

## No two children are parented the same

We bring so much of our childhood into adulthood, even tending to parent as we were parented; I know I did. And I was proud to, because I believed that my parents were great, and I asked for and willingly accepted any advice they gave. This was until I was mature enough to see that my parents only knew how to parent *me,* in their environment. They had married young and stayed together, and still love each other, whereas I was twice divorced with two children by two very different dads. I was the breadwinner and, at times, the sole carer. I was a public figure. There were so many variables at play that their parenting wisdom, which had worked on me and my sister during our time in their home, did not always fit in mine.

This made even more sense when I came across the work of Dr Gabor Maté, a renowned expert on trauma, addiction, stress and childhood. To me, his most interesting theory on parenting is his claim that no siblings ever experience the same parent.

Maté theorises that a firstborn experiences a first-time parent, filled with the worry and anxiety that all first-time parents have. A second-born child will have the benefit of a more experienced parent, who is more relaxed. They may also experience a parent who is financially more, or perhaps less, secure, with different stresses and concerns to the firstborn. And so on.[43]

Maté says that, in his experience, while we may think that we parented our children in the same way and then are confused about how and why they turn out so differently, the answers are obvious; not only are they their own person with their own idiosyncratic reactions and triggers, but they have been parented differently to their siblings. Even if all outside stimulations and factors were removed (which they never could be, but let's pretend), the children would still experience different parenting from the same mother and father, because each child also triggers a different response in each adult; a robust child evokes a different nurturing response to a more sensitive one, and each parent will have their own individual response to these factors. A daughter evokes a different response in a father, just as a son will to a mother.[44]

So, just as my parents parenting of me cannot be exactly replicated through my parenting of my children, *even my own children* will not have the same experience of me as their mother.

I know I have made mistakes with my children and will continue to. When I think back to how I parented my son compared to my daughter, from the very beginning my approach was completely different. First time around, I used a parenting book that told me to put my child in another room and let him cry himself to sleep. My heart physically hurts when I think of that now, and it is something I deeply regret. My poor, poor baby boy. I wish I had kept him close, so he felt my love and was soothed. I wonder now if that shaped a part of who he is – his independence and distance – and wish I could turn back the clock. My daughter stayed in a basket next to me for months, and I was able to easily soothe her back to sleep when needed. But she rarely needed it, and I wonder now if that is because she knew I was there, and didn't feel alone?

My family dynamics are complicated: as well as two children by two different fathers I am also a step-parent. At times I feel like I am treated as the villain of the piece, and that makes me feel misjudged and hurt. It also makes me feel unappreciated, but I know that this is how all parents feel, and that it's part of the gig. Navigating the unique wants and needs of each child, at their varying ages and stages, while also navigating our own relationship and changing circumstances is challenging. Our children have lived through my ups and downs as well as their own and have had to adapt to good times and hard times.

With hindsight, our experience of debt and loss has been our children's biggest moment of growth and learning, and an invaluable life lesson for all of us. They have seen us struggle to pay bills, work hard to keep our love and good humour going when everything was caving in, be grateful for the small wins, celebrate when moments of good fortune arrived, and work hard to find solutions when they did not. They have seen that possessions are just "things", and that selling them to meet more important needs like groceries and heating is nothing to be ashamed of. We used to go on big, expensive family holidays together; we have not had a family holiday for some years now, and it doesn't matter. If we are safe, healthy, have a roof over our heads and food in our bellies, and if we are finding work to support ourselves doing something we enjoy, then we are wealthy.

This reframing and learning could only have happened through lived experience. I am hopeful that this worst of times that we have experienced as a family has morphed into the best of times, where we have managed to hold tight and weather the storm. Obviously, the problem with this storm is that we don't know when it will end, but I hope we have taught the children that even when you cannot see the horizon, there is always hope. We can only do our best, and acknowledge that at times, as much as it hurts us, our best won't be good enough.

## Accepting the limits of good parenting

If you haven't seen the multi-Emmy Award-winning Netflix drama *Adolescence*, I would urge you to – but brace yourself for a harrowing watch. Written by Stephen Graham and Jack Thorne, it centres around the arrest of a 13-year-old boy (Jamie, played by Owen Cooper) for the murder of a girl in his school. Starring Stephen Graham as Jamie's father Eddie, what makes this drama so spectacular is that each one-hour episode was filmed using one camera, in a single take. It allows for time and space between crucial moments in ways that would happen in real time. There is no suspenseful music or sharp cutaways, it is simply a story unfolding of lives unravelling.

It is an utterly heartbreaking tale of the hidden toxic masculinity at play in our children's world that we as parents have no idea about, thinking the things we hear about online could never infiltrate our world. It is the very "normalness" of Jamie's family that makes it so harrowing. The final scene of Eddie sobbing and tucking his son's teddy bear into bed and saying "Sorry" for his unintentional and unforeseeable failings as a parent broke my heart, and doubtless others.

It was summed up in an exchange between Eddie and his wife Manda (brilliantly played by Christine Tremarco) when their elder daughter Lisa, who is a straight A student, a good girl destined for great things, but who will now always be known as "the sister of a killer", fiercely tells them they cannot move away from their home, because what has happened will always follow them. It takes their breath away, and Eddie, commenting on his daughter's strength of character and resilience, asks, "How did we make that?" and his wife replies, "The same way we made him. With love, to the best of our ability."

This was something that creator Stephen Graham felt very strongly about; he did not want the parents to be to blame. He didn't want the story to simply be a tale of a poor young boy from a dysfunctional family who does a terrible thing. This horror was felt by viewers because it could happen to all of us – yes, even us "good" parents.[45]

The drama focuses on the extreme acts of violence perpetrated on girls by young boys, and the influence on boys of controversial public figures such as Andrew Tate, the online influencer who promotes a brand of toxic masculinity predicated on dominant and manipulative behaviour. But it also centres around shame. The shame felt by young, not yet fully formed boys being rejected for not being "manly" or attractive enough to girls, and the hormonal rage felt because of it. The shame of the family for being the parents and sister of a boy who has senselessly murdered a young girl, and the consequent rejection and shaming by their community because of it. And the shame of feeling like they have failed in their roles as parents, despite their very best efforts.

The series finishes without a resolution, with no tidy ending, which makes it even more powerful. Because this is how life is. It is messy and imperfect, and we do the best we can with the knowledge and tools we are given and have learned.

Many years ago, when I first had therapy, it took me a while to tell my parents that I was seeing a therapist because I knew what their reaction would be. When I eventually told my mum, it was as I thought. "Oh my God," Mum said. "What did you say about me? You know they always blame the parents!" I understood her fear, and underneath that, her shame, that she might have her parenting dissected and be found lacking.

But none of us as parents will ever be able to raise our children and send them out into the world as fully functioning, shame-free individuals, any more than we can teach them to fly. Just as we were making it up as we went along when they were babies, we continue to do so as they grow into adulthood and beyond. Our children teach us how to parent as much as we try to teach them about the world. And just as we say to them that we love them and are proud of them for doing their best, it is all we can say to ourselves, too.

# Lessons in Becoming Shame*less* in Parenting

1. **You Are Doing the Best You Can, and That's Okay**
   I know that some people get very cross about the idea of every child being given a sticker at sports day, with no medals for coming 1st, 2nd, or 3rd. I see their point, because someone has to win at sports, and it must feel pretty crummy if you do and just get the same pat on the back as someone who came last. Winning is great, but it's not something you will ever do as a parent, which is why I think the sticker thing could actually work here.

   If your child grows up well-balanced and loving and gets a brilliant job and an OBE from the King, you'd feel pretty great, and like you've "won" at parenting. But if they didn't do any of these things, or did something that brings shame to your door, is that any more a reflection on you than their success? Parents like to take credit for the bits we get right and scratch our heads over the bits we get wrong. It is a marathon that never ends, with no crowds to cheer us on when we are flagging. So, if the kids, no matter how old they are, seem to be doing okay, then enjoy it. And if they are not, then do your best with the tools you have, and get help where you can if you need it. In this race, it is all you can do.

2. **It's Okay to Get Things Wrong**

   I have made mistakes with my parenting. None of them were deliberate, and all my actions, even those I got wrong, were done with the best of intentions. But the fallout of my decisions has impacted my children, in some cases causing hurt and pain to both them and me. I have had to accept that there is no rewind option, all we can do is acknowledge our mistakes and do better. It's never too late to say sorry, to admit you made a mistake and start again. As the 18th-century sage and poet Alexander Pope said: "To err is human, to forgive, divine",[46] and this is perhaps one of the greatest lessons that we as parents can give our children.

3. **You May Be a Parent, But You Will Always Be Somebody's Child**

   You might not appreciate this until you are much older, but you never stop being someone's baby, and they never stop being your mummy and daddy. I'm ashamed to remember that when my grandparents died, I couldn't quite understand why my parents were so upset. It was sad, and I felt upset because I loved them and liked them, but in my young mind they were old, and that was what was supposed to happen. It is only now that my parents are older that I feel the chill of fear when I think about this. I love them, and I like them, and I can't bear the thought of them not being here anymore. So, make the most of it if you are lucky enough to still have your mum and dad in your life, even if they have got things wrong, because one day your kids will have to do the same with you.

9

# NASTY GALS

*Why Shame Can Make You a Real Bitch*

*"When we judge people in areas where we're vulnerable to shame, we're often trying to protect ourselves."[47]*

Dr Brené Brown, Academic and Author

Okay. We've examined various areas of our lives where we might feel shame, so now I want to take a look what how our shame can make us react in certain situations.

At the start of this book, I talked about how the media judges and shames celebrities for failing to live up to unattainable beauty standards, and for going through something that millions of people around the world will experience – a change in financial circumstance and status. Certain parts of the media have always behaved badly and always will. Not *all* media. Responsible journalism exists and is vitally important, but there is a type of media where truth is twisted to conform to a narrative that is inflammatory, derogatory, and downright dangerous. And *social* media can be even worse, as it doesn't have to conform to the same rules that mainstream or legacy media do.

There's a reason *why* "the media" behaves the way they do. It's because people consume this stuff. And because we now don't even have to buy a newspaper or magazine to read trashy things about people, it means we can read what anyone has to say about anybody and it's all *content*. What we forget though, is that if this content is clicked on, someone, somewhere, is making money from it. It all starts with the person who uploaded it, and they are actively encouraged to put up any nonsense that gets people enraged and engaged, because more clicks mean more cash.

Who encourages them? The platform providers: the big guys at the top of the food chain, who insidiously encourage click-bait content.

They say that "Sex Sells", but to be honest, that's not entirely true. *Shame* sells more.

## Why we secretly enjoy others' misfortunes

It's horrible, but it's not surprising; social media moguls have simply found a new way to monetise something that we have been doing since the dawn of time: bitching about each other.

You might be thinking, "Whaaat? I don't do that!" But you do. We all do. It's human, it's fun, and it makes us feel part of something. It gets things off our chest and makes us feel connected to the person we're talking to. It also makes us feel relieved, because someone else has messed up or we've spotted a flaw in their "perfection"; and this is *especially true* if that person is someone we are envious of. Deep down, we know it's not nice; so why does it give us such a *frisson* of pleasure?

There is a fancy name for it: schadenfreude. It's a German word which was first used in the 18th century to describe a feeling that is as old as time. "Schaden" means harm, or damage, and "freude" means joy or pleasure. Put them together and what have you got? You have the deep pleasure that comes from witnessing another person's misfortune.

In a lighter sense, it can be giggling at a video of someone falling over; a darker version is gaining pleasure by seeing someone experience real misfortune – particularly someone we see as having a higher status to ourselves.

They say that "Sex Sells", but to be honest, that's not entirely true. *Shame* sells more

Social media may have only been around a few years, but this principle is not new. We have always done it; it's part of our DNA. You've probably heard of "Tall Poppy Syndrome". It's when we get very excited about someone, build them up, then decide that they are now a bit too full of themselves, so we tear them down again. We do it with celebrities, our peers, co-workers, and romantic partners. Such fun.

Unless it happens to you; then not so much.

We naturally compare ourselves to people we view as more successful than ourselves, whether in terms of looks, wealth, career, or romantic partnerships. We mentally build our own Pinterest board of the things we want, or wish we had, and look admiringly at those who seem to have them. How can we get what they, seemingly effortlessly, have? When we don't get them, or can't have them, for whatever reason, we can feel angry and resentful. It seems very unfair.

This is where the "fun" starts.

If we see someone else as being more successful than us, in whatever sphere, it can bring out our ugly side. We can feel jealous, and sometimes that's justified, because we try really hard while someone else seems to glide through life and get offered all these opportunities that we aren't. Maybe they are just born prettier, or smarter, or into a richer family, so they had a head start that we'll never catch up with. It feels horrible.

Now, we have two choices. We can decide that what someone else has, or is, has nothing to do with us, and crack on with our own life. Or we can keep comparing ourselves to others and wishing things were different, feeling increasingly envious, angry, and inadequate. These feelings of inadequacy are where things become interesting, because they stem from shame. You've probably heard the saying "Hurt people hurt people". It's true. If we are okay with who we are in the grand scheme of things, even allowing for wanting certain parts of our lives to be different, we find it easier to let things go.

## The dark side of comparison

If we aren't in that mental space, then this changes our perspective on everything. Because, as the deeply introspective novelist Anaïs Nin wrote: "We don't see things as they are, we see them as *we are.*"[48]

For example, I can get a teensy bit *ragey* every now and then. It's hard to imagine, I know... But I am human, so bear with me. Say one morning I sleep through my alarm and am going to be late for work. I run out the door, and everyone is walking at a snail's pace, chatting to each other and blocking my way. Rage-induced mutterings of "For God's sake, Come *on!!!*" ensue. Maybe I'm in my car, the traffic is horrendous, and every traffic light is red. I then yell at the top of my lungs, using language that would make a sailor blush. When I finally get to work, *everyone* is annoying and I swear they are being deliberately difficult. I go on to have a terrible day, am an emotional wreck by the time I get home, and I hate everything and everybody.

Isn't it funny how *other* people are the ones who are annoying, and walk too slowly, and are in the car in front, when you are running late and need to get somewhere?

Now think of this terrible day where you are late and everyone is annoying in the context of comparison and shame. Instead of accepting that you are being a little unreasonable because you're stressed, you project those feelings outwards, through criticism (bitching to your colleagues about those annoying pedestrians) or shaming (yelling out of your car window).

This is an example of how we react and behave on a single day when things aren't going so great, and it can be understood and excused because we all have days like these, where emotions are heightened. But what happens when we feel like this *every* day, on a simmering, low-level scale that we don't notice because it has become a part of who we are? When wanting to level the playing field so that either everyone feels as bad as we do, or seeing someone brought down a peg or two so that we feel better, has become part of our internal makeup, without us even noticing?

This is when we internally and externally start to justify how we are feeling. We perceive arrogance where perhaps there is none. We feel that people are underserving of their success because they don't appreciate it as much as we would, or they aren't humble about it, as we would be.

Those feelings of schadenfreude are understandably intensified on a day when we're raging at the world, especially if that person is someone we feel a little shitty towards. That internal, "Ha! Not so clever now, are we?" feels good. It makes us feel better.

If we are part of a group that does this (whether that's via WhatsApp, coffee chat, or an online pile-on) then these feelings are magnified and the joy rockets! There is something quite heady about being part of a gang that slags off an outsider who has what we do not: it taps into our tribal sense of belonging. "It's alright for *them*," we moan together as the people we are talking about lose any sense of humanness in our eyes. They become "other". They are so unlike us that they can't possibly feel pain or hurt, which helps negate any feelings of guilt, remorse, or shame that we may feel because of our actions towards them.

We can all be "judgy" of each other, we just do it in different ways and for different reasons. But *why?* And is it something that both men and women do equally?

## The psychology of shaming others

Psychologically, shaming often serves a social function. According to Thomas J Scheff, the American sociologist known for his pioneering work on shame, emotions, and social bonds, shame is a "social emotion" that holds societies together.[49] It can form a unifying bond, forging a sense of belonging to "us" while uniting against "them". It makes us feel part of something, and we all know that we are stronger as a species if we stand together, even in something that is negative, like shaming.

I believe that, for men, shaming usually stems from a desire for dominance, being in competition with someone who threatens the hierarchy. Think of how strong group elders or leaders will jostle for position and use power play to maintain control. It is not new, and if we look back through the evolution of our species, men have been expected to be brave, strong, independent, and successful – qualities that will have meant different things at different times, but the premise is the same. It means that when a man seemingly fails to meet those standards, he is shamed by other men, and occasionally also by women.

For women, shaming has also tended to be about maintaining social order within their own hierarchy, making sure everyone cooperates and gets along, and supports each other.

Like anything, it works when it works. But any outliers who don't conform to the rules and norms laid down by that society make the rest feel on edge. What are they doing? Why aren't they behaving like you're supposed to? *What's wrong with them?* And shaming begins. It can stem from a fear of this different behaviour and insecurity that they pose a threat. But it can also come from jealousy, because they may make people feel inadequate. Perhaps the man is *too* independent and strong, so he should be taken down because he could challenge the status quo. Perhaps the woman is *too* beautiful and popular and might attract attention from a married mate. A perceived rival needs to be shamed and destroyed.

It's why we love to watch TV dramas like *Succession* or *The White Lotus;* it makes us feel good to think that people who are beautiful, rich, and successful beyond our wildest dreams, who have everything we could ever want, are actually desperately unhappy, riddled with insecurity, and want to rip each other apart. Pass the popcorn, we want to see this!

While it's fun to watch it play out via a fictional character on TV, schadenfreude takes on a whole different energy when something that has happened in real life goes viral online, where someone we will never meet is scandalised or even cancelled. The consequences for those involved are far from entertaining. It's not social media's *fault* that we feel the way we do about people who seem to "have it all", but our participation in tearing them down has now changed dramatically since its inception. Because now it's not simply about enjoying someone's downfall from afar – we now play an active part in it.

The biggest shift that we have seen in public shaming is that rather than it simply happening at the level of the village stocks, we now metaphorically throw rotten food at a perceived wrong doer on a global scale, as anything posted online has the potential of reaching an unlimited audience, unfettered by geography. There is no escaping the wrath of the misinformed, or the willingly enraged, and it doesn't simply disappear once the surge of collective emotion recedes.

It can happen in a moment: one minute you are in each other's arms at a concert and the next you are being shown on the big screen, and a whole stadium sees you freeze in shock, then pull away and hide your face; the lead singer sees your reaction and laughingly comments that perhaps you're shy or having an affair? It's caught on someone's mobile phone, they upload the footage and BOOM! Life as you know it is over.

It is unsettling to accept, but if we watch and comment and share, then we are taking part in the machine that is shaming another human. The video that gets a million views happens because a *million* individuals, just like you and me, decided to watch it. A like, a share, a thoughtless shitty comment, or an intentionally hurtful one, becomes part of another human's downfall.

The 2025 documentary series *Caroline Flack: Search for the Truth* chronicles the suicide of British TV presenter Caroline Flack, featuring her mother Christine discussing the events that led to her daughter's death. As Christine explains in an interview with *Vanity Fair* magazine,[50] the build-up to Caroline's suicide was the perfect storm of a vulnerable person in the spotlight being prosecuted and publicly shamed for behaviour that was not only mis-reported, but also repeatedly exaggerated.

The barrage of misleading and inflammatory reporting in the lead up to Caroline's death fed the fire of cruel online trolling, which, according to her mother, Caroline read and was deeply affected by.[51] She was vilified as a human being and could not see a way to come back from the shame of it.

In the truly tragic case of Caroline Flack, she was horrifically publicly shamed for something in her present. But it doesn't even have to be a current error of judgement that causes a pile-on, it can be something that was said or done in the past. Nowadays it could be from 20 years ago, when Facebook first appeared and Twitter was just a micro-blogging site and people didn't realise the permanency of what they said or did, or were just young, dumb, and showing off. It can now be dug up and played out in the court of public opinion, and outrage can be whipped up in moments. Every click, comment, and share pours more fuel onto the fire until it is out of control and the person engulfed in it is burnt to a crisp.

But if this behaviour of shaming others is a human instinct, surely it's not our fault, especially if it's now being manipulated by algorithms and those in charge of them?

Absolutely. But just because something is a human instinct it doesn't mean we are powerless against it. We have simply slid into the habit of thinking that what we do doesn't have an impact. It may feel that way, because we don't meet the person we are criticising or commenting on, and we don't see the resulting fallout of our actions. But when we make a nasty comment under someone's post or create a horrible video about them, it's a real person who receives it. That can lead to stress, anxiety, unwanted and disturbing thoughts, and – in some tragic cases – suicide. Our behaviour has been a contributing factor in the occurrence of this event.

## Becoming desensitised

The idea that ordinary people will go against their better nature and deliberately cause others pain is also not a new discovery but formed part of a social psychology experiment carried out at Yale University in 1961 by Stanley Milgram.[52] He initially wanted to measure the willingness of participants to obey an authority figure who instructed them to behave in a way that was against their personal conscience. It was a simple experiment; participants were asked to administer increasingly painful electric shocks to someone in another room when that person answered questions incorrectly. Unknown to them, this other person was an actor and was not in fact receiving any shocks.

The predicted result was that only 0.1% of participants would administer the maximum level of shocks, which was a painful and dangerous 450 volts, and that most would refuse once they heard the person's cries and suffering. This was not what happened. A staggering 65% administered the full 450 volts, and 100% administered at least 300 volts – enough to cause considerable pain.

The results overwhelmingly showed that people who would never normally behave this way will follow authority figures, even to the point of causing significant harm to an innocent person. The results also concluded that they are *more* willing to do this if they are relieved of the responsibility for the other person's pain.

It proved that if someone can reframe the suffering they are knowingly causing an innocent person in a way that means their actions are "not their fault", then they quickly become desensitised and will keep doing it to maximum effect.

Obviously, social media was not around when this experiment was conducted, but the correlation between removal of responsibility between action and reaction would surely be the same. We have become so desensitised by the ready opportunities to anonymously and repeatedly cause someone pain that we don't see a problem with it. And we can justify it by reframing it as "they had it coming".

I don't always look at the profiles of people who troll me online, but when I do there is a similarity to them. The women are often pictured with their children and grandchildren, with the tagline "Be Kind. Live, Love, Laugh" under their photo. The men have photos with their wives and/or children.

These people no doubt love their families very much and would be devastated if someone hurt them. And yet they happily, and willingly, with no coercion, either with intentional malice or without much forethought, write terrible things directly to a person they have never met, specifying the kind of harm they want to befall them or calling them horrible names. Because there is a separation of cause and effect, a desensitisation to the pain it will cause, and a removal of blame because "everyone does it", it doesn't seem like a big deal.

Of course, this has always happened in real life too. When it does, we call it bullying, as that's what this behaviour is, whether it's happening in school, at work, or in a friendship group. Using the word "trolling" downplays the problem.

What do *I* think causes this behaviour? I could name many things, but top of the list would be shame and not feeling "good enough". As Dr Brené Brown suggested in the quote at the start of this chapter, our criticism of others often stems from fear of our own shortcomings and wanting to distance ourselves from these.

Shame doesn't care what we have, or what we do for a living, and can manifest in anger, defensiveness, and aggression. In other words, it can make us a real bitch, both online and offline.

So, what if you're recognising yourself as a person who is shaming others? What if shame has made *you* act like someone you don't want to be?

## Facing uncomfortable truths

Life can be challenging for everyone. We know this. But online life, this strange place where things don't seem real, can be a bit much. What we see online can trigger our shame response without us even knowing that's what is happening: we compare, we feel a failure, rejected, and criticised, even if that's not actually what's happening. This is because we are reacting in one of three possible ways:

- We are hyper-*defensive* and feel like everything is an attack.
- We are hyper-*offensive* and feel like everything is a target.
- We are emotionally flooded and don't see the nuance of a situation, so everything becomes a big deal, even if it's not.

Do any of these ring true for you? If so, maybe it's time for you to step away from your phone for a while and think about how you're acting and reacting in real life as well.

It is not a nice feeling when we realise that, actually, *we* are behaving badly. I know I didn't like it when I realised my husband was right about me being negative all the time, even though I had lots of reasons to be. When I was sick and struggling to find positivity in anything, I would notice *all* the bad stuff. Every annoying cyclist cutting us up in traffic was cause for a lengthy rant; every dog poo in the street that an owner had left for someone to step in would get me going (although, there is a special place in hell for people who don't pick up after their pet, and I'm not backing down on that one); every bit of banter that he instigated was shot down because I didn't find *anything* funny. But having lots of reasons to be badly behaved doesn't excuse the behaviour. And thinking, "But hey, we're all human" will only go so far, especially if we really have broken House Rule Number One: Don't Be A Dick.

If you've realised that shame has made you behave like a nasty gal, the first thing to do is congratulate yourself for realising and accepting it, because you are now already way ahead of most people. Now do something about it. Start by figuring out why it's happened. Here's what I do when I need to get to the bottom of something like this; see if it works for you.

Shame doesn't care what we have, or what we do for a living, and can manifest in anger, defensiveness, and aggression. In other words, it can make us a real bitch

- Sit quietly with a notebook, or open the notes app on your phone, somewhere that you won't be disturbed. Ask yourself, "Why am I behaving like this?"
- Something will come to mind, and whatever it is, jot it down. Then ask yourself, "But why?" Once again, make a note of whatever comes into your mind.
- Then ask yourself: "But why?" Write down the answer that comes into your mind, and then do it again. And again.

Asking yourself "Why?" and noting your answer, then asking "why" underneath that answer, and the next, and the next, is an extremely useful tool for digging down to the root of the things. The reason you ask yourself "Why?" five times is because the true reason is never what comes up in the first why. Your mind is clever and sly, and it is trying to protect you from thinking about something deeply unpleasant, so it takes the removal of a few layers of subterfuge before you get anywhere close to the truth.

Another great method is this simple question, which I have used countless times when coaching clients and listening to friends talking about things that are really troubling them. It is especially useful when you can't think why you have done something out of character or why something has gone so wrong. You, or they, might be saying, "I just don't know why I do this/ what to do/where to begin!" Now ask yourself, or them, "But if you *did* know, what do you think the answer would be?"

You see, deep down, we often know the answers, we just don't want to look at them because they are uncomfortable or they make us feel ashamed. Facing any uncomfortable truth is hard, but it is a vital part of moving on from any behaviour that doesn't serve us, even if that behaviour is our own.

If it is *you* that is the victim of nasty gal (or nasty guy) behaviour, you don't need to suffer in silence. We often don't even recognise bullying when it happens as adults; we call it a number of different things: gossip, undermining, passive-aggressive remarks. Labelling it as what it truly is, which is bullying or shaming, takes away much of its power, because it means it is not you who is being weak, it is them who are behaving badly.

While calling them out may not seem to be an option, particularly if they are doing it within your friendship group and you don't want to "make a fuss", that's never a reason to not address it.

The following practical steps will hopefully give you some guidance if it is happening to you.

* Ask them when you are alone if they are aware of what they are doing and tell them how they are making you feel. They will most likely deny it, but now they cannot pretend they are unaware.
* Don't let shame silence you: tell a friend, partner, or colleague and let them support you. It will help you feel less alone and embarrassed. Let them fight your corner if it helps; they can report what's happening or respond in a measured way.
* With online shaming, document *everything*: screenshot what they've said and keep a folder of evidence. If it's on Snapchat, which will show that you are documenting what they are sending, it's up to you if you'd prefer to screenshot and let them know, or take photos of your screen using someone else's phone, so they don't know.
* Report, block, delete: I do this all the time. I don't engage, because that's what they want. Block, report, delete, and carry on with your day. If things get really bad, consider making your account private.
* Take a break from social media: it's not helpful to keep poking the wound and wondering why it won't heal. Have a break, or, if you must have a little peek, use a friend's phone and look up stuff that makes you feel good, and *do not* check your profile. If you need to keep your account active because it's part of your job, then ask someone to take over for a while.

- Reframe the shame: it feels like this shaming is about you, but it's not. It says a lot more about the person doing it than it does about you. Don't take it personally, either. Just because someone is saying something about you, doesn't make it true.

# Lessons in Changing Nasty Gal Habits

1. **You Don't See Things as They Are, You See Them as You Are**

   Feeling furious with the world has only a little bit to do with the world itself. Yes, some things are terrible, and annoying, and unfair, but they have always been that way and will continue to be that way, regardless. While it is extremely irritating to have someone tell you to chill out about things that wind you up, they kind of have a point. This doesn't mean that you can't feel jealous of someone who seems to have it much easier than you – I mean, you're right, that's so annoying! But what good is being a bitch about it? It won't change their fortunes, and it certainly won't change yours. Let's try and remind ourselves that we are seeing the world as we are, not how it is. We can give ourselves a minute to reflect on it (aka sulk), then make a change.

2. **Step Away From Your Triggers or Someone Is Going to Get Hurt**

   In the first instance, it's someone else who gets hurt, as you lash out and say something or do something horrible. This feels good for a moment, but afterwards only feeds into our sense of shame and self-loathing, even if that's buried under a few defensive layers. That means the second person to get hurt is *you*.

If someone or something is making you react in a way that you're not proud of, or that you wouldn't teach your kids to do, then stay away from them. That dopamine hit from scrolling online and saying nasty, nasty things to people you don't even know feels amazing and is addictive, especially the longer you do it and "get away" with it. But you're doing the equivalent of drinking poison while hoping the other person dies. Ask yourself why you are behaving as you are, and if the answer is something that you think you will need help to overcome, then ask for it. There is no shame in that.

3. **Don't Be a Dick**
It's not cool. Enough said.

# 10

# YOU'RE A LONG TIME DEAD

*Embracing Ugly Truths to Live a Shameless Life*

*"I'm so grateful for the girl that went through those things, went through that situation. Because now, I'm the woman that I am because of her."*[53]

Ella Langley, *Country Music Singer Songwriter*

I am a sucker for country music. There is always a message of love and hope in among the tales of woe, whiskey, and wronged women that warms my heart. My parents loved this kind of music, and we spent many a car journey singing along to John Denver, Glen Campbell, and Don McLean – whom I once told some classmates I was the daughter of, to explain why I'd moved around so much.

One of my dad's favourite songs is "Friends In Low Places" by Garth Brooks. He'd play it at top volume, and we'd all join in and sing along as loudly as we could. He loved dropping my kids off at school when they were little, blasting it out and timing it so they were all singing it as the car pulled up at the gates. They still talk about it now.

## Learn to take the rough with the smooth

I think that country music makes everything feel okay because, no matter what we are going through, someone has either been through it and come out the other side, or penned witty lyrics to make it seem all right. My current favourite country music star is Ella Langley, who in her young and fresh way captures emotions that my middle-aged heart recognises and warms to. Because that's the thing about life; we're all on a bumpy journey through it. We may as well accept that, as much as we'd love a smooth ride, it's the rough that toughens us up, or at the very least makes us interesting. Things won't work out, hearts will break, and there will be many disappointments along the way, especially if you are brave enough to keep trying.

One of the reasons I wanted to share my stories with you in this book was to show you that life is about trying and failing, and trying and succeeding, and you can't have one without the other. There are so many things that you won't be able to do, that won't work out, but that's where the greatest learnings lie. Which is deeply annoying, because wouldn't it be so much easier and less messy if the learnings were simply found in cute memes or Instagram quotes?

What's the point in all this failure, this thing that we have been indoctrinated to think is the worst possible outcome of any endeavour? Whether it is revealing our true feelings and having them ridiculed, attempting something only for it to go wrong, or losing our money and status, the point of it all is to learn and grow, and to build our resilience and strength while doing so. It really is all about the journey and not the destination.

I see this so clearly now when I look at my own parents, who have had a full and exciting life and are still up for finding adventure and purpose, while accepting the limitations that their age and physical health have placed upon them. Accepting what you can and cannot do, and having the passion and resilience to keep going is surely what a life well lived is all about. You are a long time dead, so making the life you have worth living *has* to be the point of it all.

If there is one good thing that comes from repeated struggles, it is this: knowing, somewhere deep inside, that you have it within you to cope. This knowing is sometimes fleeting, and it can come in a flash of "Dammit, yes I can! I have survived before, and I will do it again!" But surrounding this self-knowledge, like a barbed wire cage, is the shame that you are here again, and the fear that perhaps this time you will not recover from it. Perhaps *this* is the thing that you will not recover from.

This is where resilience comes in.

All those years ago, when I took part in *SAS: Who Dares Wins*, I was taken to the mountains of Chile and put through my paces by ex-SAS and SBS officers. It was brutal, leading to the resurfacing of supressed emotions from experiences I had pushed down to the depths of me, and eventually to a breakdown. I now see that challenging time, which in many ways changed the course of my life, as a breakthrough, something many people who have had similar experiences agree can be the case.

There were plenty of positives, not least getting to meet these incredible men and hear their stories. They are tough cookies who have an ability to withstand pain and discomfort at a level us mere mortals can't quite comprehend. Having had the privilege of getting to know them afterwards, I've gained a greater understanding of why they are so hard on the show's participants: not least because they want to recreate as accurately as possible the sheer grit that is needed to pass SAS selection, but also because they know it's not simply about being strong. It's about what you can withstand when you are far outside your comfort zone, fully consumed by pain and fear, and don't know how long you are expected to take it for.

## Building shameless resilience

We can all put up with uncomfortable experiences. We have done it; from a punishing HIIT class at the gym to gritting your teeth while getting your legs waxed. At a very basic level, this is about endurance and resilience because you want a result.

But what about resilience in the face of something life-changing, like debt? Or ill health? Or a dysfunctional relationship? Or challenging parenting? We can all take a deep breath and cope with short bursts of mental and physical discomfort or pain, when we can see the end goal and know it will soon be over. But what about when you can't make sense of what's happening to you, can't think of a solution to it, and have no idea when it is going to end? How do you find resilience then?

This is where the idea of shameless resilience comes in, of not allowing the circumstances of a challenge to batter you down. Even if, in fact *especially* if your situation seems insurmountable. I strongly encourage you to watch the film *Nyad*, which tells the incredible story of Diana Nyad's continued attempts to swim the 110-mile shark-infested waters of the Straits of Florida, from Cuba to the US.

Diana's resilience in the face of repeated failure is one of the standouts of her story. She attempted to do the seemingly impossible not once, but multiple times, while much of the sporting world belittled and shamed her. Her critics were harsh and vocal and continue to this day.

Her first attempt was at the age of 28.

Her age when she finally achieved it?

64.

She is, to date, the only person to have completed the swim from Cuba to Florida without a shark cage. I can't even begin to contemplate the resilience needed to stay in shark-infested waters for one second, never mind to keep swimming, without any buoyancy aid or assistance from another person, in the terrifying dark of night, fighting the Gulf Stream current, through smacks of deadly box jellyfish, for *53 hours*.

How did Diana manage to swim without drowning? In an interview with CNN the day after her epic achievement in

September 2013, her face still swollen and weather-beaten from her efforts, Diana said, "My whole mantra this year was 'Find A Way'. You don't like it, it's not doing well, *find a way*."[54]

After any incredible achievement, it is our habit to simplify and neatly package it into soundbites about grit and perseverance. We smooth over the jagged edges of effort once the pain has gone and talk eloquently about the learning and the journey. Diana's TED talk[55] about her achievement has had almost seven million views on YouTube, and it is a masterclass in never giving up – even when you are stung by poisonous jellyfish, vomiting out seawater, and hallucinating that you can see the Taj Mahal.

But how do you "find a way" when you are *metaphorically* all at sea? How do you keep going when nothing is working? When you've run out of ideas? When every single door you've tried is shut? When you are so consumed by the shame of your failure that you don't know what to do next?

There was a moment during *SAS: Who Dares Wins* when I was required to fall backwards out of a helicopter at great height, to land headfirst into a cold lake in the Andes mountains. Yes, it was as painful as it sounds. Don't try this at home.

I followed my instructions – the parts I could hear over the deafening din of the helicopter and my thudding heart – closed my eyes and let myself fall. The impact when I hit the water was like falling onto wet concrete. My head felt like it would burst with pain, and I opened my eyes to see nothing but brown water and bubbles. I instinctively righted myself and swam to the surface, my army boots filling with water and my sweatshirt becoming heavier by the second.

As I burst through the surface, my face contorted into ugly crying with pain and shock. For around 15 seconds.

Then I turned and swam to shore and the waiting cameras, my face showing nothing at all.

How could anyone do that? This is when resilience is a form of survival. It comes with knowing that crying is a momentary release, but it will do you no good in the long run to continue, so you stop.

This is what repeated failure teaches you: that pain is transitory, it will pass; that lying down and simply crying without taking action is pointless. Like Diana Nyad, ploughing her way through jellyfish and ocean currents, it means pushing your past behind you and pulling your future towards you, one stroke at a time.

If you are going through something now and are simply trying to stay afloat, then I send you my love and sympathy. And I'd urge you to have your moment where you cry, rage, and howl at the moon when you need to – but then ask yourself, "Now what can I *do*?"

We all know the saying "This Too Shall Pass". It is useful to keep handy when times are terrible *and* when times are great, to remind ourselves that all our experiences are transitory, whether we like them very much or not at all. Some things must simply be endured, they cannot be avoided, no matter how much we wish they could.

Would I do things differently had I known how painful the last few years would be because of decisions I made? Yes. I made mistakes with my business that I wish I had not. But perhaps I was supposed to make them. Perhaps there was a lesson I needed to learn, or a path I needed to be on that I would not otherwise have found. I will never know, and there is little point in musing over the "what ifs" because this is where I find myself now.

Where is the good? What *have* I learnt? Gratitude is the most obvious one. I have always appreciated everything I've had. I enjoyed having a good salary and feeling safe and comfortable, being able to provide for my children and take care of myself. I loved knowing I could help family members who were struggling or treat them to nice things to make them feel better. I liked the feeling of helping and being kind. But I took for granted that it would always be this way, until I lost it all and felt the shame of debt.

In much the same way, I appreciated that I was fit and strong because I went to the gym and ate well, and I liked that I looked good. But again, I failed to appreciate it until I got really sick. Losing strength, muscle, and tone in my body stopped mattering when I needed it to simply work, to keep me alive.

I have to remind myself of these things when I look in the mirror sometimes. I don't have the material things I once had. I don't look how I used to look. But I will be a long time dead – something my experience of illness taught me – so I am grateful for what I have *now*.

Could I have made better life decisions? Of course, couldn't we all? Did I learn from them? Abso-bloody-lutely. And so did my children, the very people I wanted to give a comfortable life to. They learnt to fend for themselves, that nothing lasts forever, and to appreciate what we have, when we have it. They got jobs to help them pay their way and learnt the value of things for themselves in a way that I could not have shown them. I see now that my desire to give them comfort was not a gift: it was all they knew, and they had no point of comparison to realise that they were blessed – and me telling them so didn't count. We need to feel adversity, really experience it, before we understand. And they did.

I remember one Saturday afternoon when Nick found an old wallet while sorting through a box. We were in the depths of our most challenging time and were having to sell our belongings to pay bills. Inside the wallet was £60. It felt like we had won the lottery! We discussed what to do with it. Put it towards a bill? We decided no, instead we would treat ourselves to something we hadn't had for the longest time – a Chinese takeaway. The excitement of going through the menu and the buzz when the delivery arrived felt like nothing we'd experienced before. Previously, ordering a takeaway was done without a thought, we all took it for granted. This evening, nothing had ever tasted so sweet.

## A new hope

As we come to the end of this book, I want to leave you with hope. I am not out the other side of my experience, safely, neatly, and patronisingly able to tell you that I'm so smart, I've figured out the answers to all my problems. Not at all. But I hope that I have shown you some useful, practical ways to build the resilience you need to work through any shame that you are experiencing, and given you a perspective on it that you may not have considered before.

As I mentioned at the outset, one of the things that comes with being a person in the public eye is that I have been publicly shamed more times than I care to remember. Sometimes it's things that have been completely made up by journalists; one front-page corker was that Nick threatened to leave me unless we adopted a baby. I fact-checked this story with the two people who would know if it was true or not (Nick and me) and yup, completely false. Sometimes I've been shamed because of my looks: too thin, too fat, too "done", or I've "let myself go". Sometimes because of my actions. But sometimes I have been shamed because of things that were completely out of my control.

I'd like to end this book with one of my most surreal experiences, which was when I was unwittingly caught up in a multi-million-pound scandal that made the news *around the world*.

I had been asked to star in a low-budget British gangster film called *Landscape of Lies* (an apt title, as it turned out). I wasn't, and am not, an actress, but I was asked to audition, so I did, and I got the part. I figured "Why not?" I played the part of a bisexual serial-killing therapist, which was a lot of fun as it was clearly nothing like me in real life. The team were great, the crew were lovely, the other actors were brilliantly supportive, and I enjoyed my few days of filming. I did it and then went back to my day job, and that was that.

Until a year or so later, when the editor of *Loose Women* rang to see if I was okay. Nervously I asked why, as nothing untoward had happened that day. She asked if I'd seen the papers. I hadn't, and my heart sank, because that normally means one thing – that I'd lost my job and this was how I'd find out (yes, that really happens).

I grabbed my laptop and clicked on the Mail Online. There it was: a headlining story about "Andrea McLean in £3 million tax fraud scandal".[56]

Whaaaat?!! Yup, me and the other actors, the writer, and crew had been part of a film that was funded by fraudsters. The perpetrators ended up going to prison, and the story went global. The BBC made a documentary about it, how criminals had fraudulently claimed grants and tax benefits for a film they never intended to make, then once they realised they were going to be found out quickly funded a small movie and hoped to cover their tracks. The documentary is called *The Great Gangster Film Fraud* and is worth a watch.[57]

Did I feel shame because of this? Well, I felt pretty stupid for being caught up in it and my name being used for splashy headlines. But honestly? I was more embarrassed that my terrible acting was now available for scrutiny around the world. Something that I'd thought was fun to try and wouldn't get much attention didn't quite turn out that way. But I wasn't ashamed because I didn't do anything wrong. And I'm glad it was made clear that the writer and the team had nothing to do with the tax swindle, as they were decent people who just wanted to do a good job. Like many potentially shameful episodes, it's become an entertaining story to share. This was simply a moment to chalk up to experience and add to the list of things that could have gone better.

The feelings of despair and hopelessness that I had when I simultaneously lost my business and my health were much darker, and are feelings that most of us will experience, for our own reasons. At some point in our lives, we will undergo what is known as a "dark night of the soul", a term taken from the poem of this name by the 16th-century Catholic mystic St John of the Cross.[58]

It is used to describe a time of crisis, existential or otherwise, where everything we placed meaning upon is shattered, leaving us in a confusing space where nothing makes sense. It can happen at the end of a relationship or following the loss of a job, in fact everything I have written about in this book, and of course much more. It is anything that causes us to feel disconnected from ourselves and who we are – anything that brings us shame.

Psychologically, this is seen as a vital time in our personal development, because rather than simply being a moment where everything goes "wrong", it is a moment where things also have the opportunity to go "right".

How often has hindsight shown you that the destruction you faced was actually a blessing in disguise? Not all blessings come in comfortable packages, like a lottery win to relieve our financial strain; sometimes they happen in horrific ways.

The benefit of your dark night of the soul could be that you are now able to share your experience to help others and salve some of their pain. I believe that has been the biggest blessing I have taken from all my experiences. I see now that they were meant to happen, not just to help me shape shift and grow, but to pass on my learnings so that other people can make sense of what they are experiencing and do the same.

Your dark night will be unique to you; for Diane Nyad it was trying for 36 years to do the impossible, against incredible odds, to fulfil a need very few can understand and many tried to shame her for. Her achievement means that millions can emulate her shameless resilience in the face of resistance to strike out on their own, even when the odds are stacked against them.

For me, as for many, I have had repeated dark nights of the soul, and each has provided me with a breakthrough and a learning that I will carry with me until the next one. I know there will be others, and I accept that, as I hope you will too.

My hope is that you can see that challenging experiences do not define you. Self-love and acceptance help us understand that shame is simply trying to protect us, to keep us safe and connected, but also that it can at times be too powerful to be useful. By showing ourselves the same love and compassion that we would offer a friend, we can learn to accept that even if our situation is awful, it does not mean that *we* are.

# Lessons in Becoming Shame*less* in Life

1. **Adapt to Change**
   The greatest cause of stress is wishing that people, things, or circumstances were different to how they are. I know this is one of my greatest weaknesses, and I have wasted so much time feeling angry about things I cannot change. I have learnt to pause, take a breath, and remind myself that wishing it were not so will not change anything. Then I ask, how can I adjust my mindset, behaviour, and actions to help me adapt? How can I take control and not focus on the negative? It's hard, and I don't always remember to do it, and I certainly don't always get it right. But I have an awareness that I did not have before, and when I am able to catch myself in time, it has saved me from frustration and pain.

   You can never know what another decision would have led to. You think afterwards, "If only I had done this or that instead, everything would be different." But it may not have been. It may have been even worse! You will *never know*; you can only own the decision you made.

2. **Be Accountable**
   If you've messed up, own it. Be honest about it to yourself and others. Wishing you hadn't done something, wishing you had made a different decision or chosen a different path does

not remove you from the path you are on. Remember Salma Hyak's words: it is your mistake, so own it. You are not the first person to screw up, and you won't be the last, so stop making it such a big deal. If others want to make a big deal about it that's up to them, but find a way to make peace with it in your own mind. Make amends, make changes, and make progress. Otherwise, it will all have been for nothing.

Do what you say you're going to do. We'd never break a promise that we make to a friend or loved one, and yet we break the promises we make to ourselves every day. This teaches us that we cannot rely on ourselves, so we don't trust our intuition or our decisions because that small voice in our head whispers, "Why should I believe you? You never follow through." This allows us to be easily led, and misled, because we start ignoring our gut instincts. Start small, so that the promises are easy, and you feel good keeping them. Often, we start off too big – think of all the New Year's resolutions that have crashed and burned before the end of January. This is not about being bold, it is about building the habit of keeping a promise to yourself and taking small steps before progressing to bigger ones. I guarantee you will feel good if you do this.

3. **Face Your Feelings**
Shame makes you feel awful about yourself, and you are the only one who can make that stop. The way to do this is to face your feelings; don't push them down or ignore them, or try to throw them onto someone else, as tempting as that is. I've been known to be grumpy when I'm feeling bad about myself, and it takes a strong relationship to put up with that and tell me that what I am doing is unfair on myself and everyone else. If someone is letting you know that you are being a bit of a bitch, maybe they are onto something? Take a

long, hard look at yourself and face what you are feeling, then work out how you can change it.

When things fall apart, or you have been publicly shamed, there is nothing else to do but accept it. You can rage, fight, howl, and cry, but you must accept that it has happened, even if you don't agree with it. All that matters is how *you* deal with this, not how others react to it. A healthy ego understands this, so if this is what you struggle with the most when something goes wrong in your life, perhaps it's time for an ego health check. If you are secure in your sense of who you are, know your strengths and limitations, and are aware of your worth without the need for validation from others, then you can withstand the storm of public scrutiny.

Life isn't fair, but it is glorious. It isn't fair if you were born in a country with safe running water and a roof over your head, and an education and health system that is free, while others were not. It isn't fair if you are able to think and move freely, while others cannot. We tend to think that unfairness only works in one direction – the one that is against us – but that's not so. Spending a moment to recognise how much you have, and take for granted, that others do not, is worth the time that often we do not give it.

# EPILOGUE

*OMG, You're SHAMELESS!*

> *"We must accept finite disappointment,*
> *but never lose infinite hope."*[59]

*Martin Luther King Jr, Civil Rights Activist and Political Philosopher*

We all love a happy ending. Whether it's in a romantic comedy, a crazy thriller, or our own life story, we just want to know that it will all be all right in the end.

But that's the thing about life versus movies – you never know when the end is. You don't know if the shitstorm you're in is where you'll finish up, or if it's just a transitional period. You don't ever really know the full extent of what you're dealing with. Does this good fortune I'm experiencing mean that it's finally all over and I can breathe again? Is it all going to be okay? Or is another dumpster on fire about to appear around the corner to run me over?

You just don't know, which is why you have to take the wins when you get them, and acknowledge them.

Today was a win. I rang my credit card company to tell them that, after two years of selling my possessions, cashing in my pension, scaling down my life so that my outgoings were as minimal as possible, and thankfully being able to work around my illness, I was finally able to pay off my balance. I was no longer in debt to them or anyone else.

This doesn't mean I am somehow flush with money; God no. I still have a way to go. But it means that from today, anything I earn will go towards bills, living expenses and, please God, *savings* for the first time in years.

I'd never spoken to the woman on the phone before, but she obviously had my notes in front of her and knew the trouble we'd been in for the past few years. She asked a series of questions about my circumstances, including if I was able to cover bills. I said yes, "I have paid off all my loans. Paying this now means I'm officially debt-free." As the words left my mouth, I felt myself choke up.

"Oh!" she exclaimed. "That's *fantastic* news, I'm so happy for you! Huge congratulations! This must have been such a stressful time for you. Well done for getting yourself back on track, that is a huge achievement." She sounded genuinely happy for me, and a little emotional herself. I felt tears prick my eyes.

That's the thing about being in debt. It's so shameful that you don't tell family or friends that you're struggling, which means you end up in even more difficulty, as I did. The shame that keeps you quiet also means that when you do manage to make it, exhausted and battered, to the shore, there is no one there to congratulate you for what is probably your biggest life achievement. You didn't drown. Somehow, you kept swimming, and you made it.

While I have been writing this book, I have done what I can to create a space where I view the problems I face as simply life's natural challenges, the kind that all of us will face. Aside from working hard and smart to make sure I *never* end up in debt again, this involves doing what I can to keep my relationships with those I love in a happy place. It means doing this with my husband, having survived the fallout of our most challenging time as a couple. Doing the same with my children as they navigate young adulthood, and with my parents in their twilight years.

And above all, doing this with myself. It means finding a loving acceptance of who and what I am now. To some, I am "That

The shame that keeps you quiet also means that when you do manage to make it, exhausted and battered, to the shore, there is no one there to congratulate you for what is probably your biggest life achievement woman whose star has faded", and there's not much I can do about that. To me, deep inside, I am the woman who is not afraid to take a deep breath and start all over again.

I have taken another risk and made another leap of faith. I see now that this is something I am destined to repeat, and I am okay with that. I now know that I cannot fly; I have the scars to prove it, so this leap has allowed for some bounce. And if again I fall to the earth, I know I can survive, because I have done so before.

I have now sold the rest of my worldly belongings. The things and stuff that made up my life. The kitchen table where we sat as a family. The couch where we watched TV. The good wine glasses that were rarely used, the side tables, the bookshelves, the bed, my clothes... They are gone, because I am now travelling light.

I am empty nesting, but on my own terms. I am leaving everything (but not everyone) behind to start again in the sunshine. I will take my learnings with me as I leave my old life behind and prepare to begin again. I have no idea if this new adventure will work, but I know there is no shame in trying. This leap of faith is not something that everyone will understand or approve of, but this doesn't concern me.

I intend to squeeze every last beautiful drop out of the life I have been given, and to be completely and utterly *shameless* while doing so. I hope I have given you the courage to do the same.

# Acknowledgements

This book would never have happened if it wasn't for Adrian Sington and Alice Welby at Kruger Cowne. Having never met them before, I emailed and asked for a meeting as I had an idea I wanted to pitch to them. They sat down with me, we had a chat, and I went away and put together the first few chapters and a synopsis of what would eventually become this book. I emailed it over, and spent the next few weeks nervously nail biting and checking my inbox. Was I out of my mind to want to write about something so raw and exposing? Was it "too much"? Finally, a reply from Adrian: "This is f***ing brilliant Andrea. I love it." To which I promptly burst into tears.

Alice, you have been a constant source of encouragement throughout this whole process, pushing me to release the rebel inside, who is somewhat hidden underneath my good girl leanings.

To everyone at DK Red, who saw promise in that first pitch and have helped me shape this into something coherent and powerful: Elizabeth, Fritha, Jasmin, Liza and Gaynor, thank you for your feedback, questions, suggestions, and changes, all of which have made this book what it was meant to be.

To my lovely family: Betty and Jack (Mum and Dad) and my sister Linda, who have held me together through the most challenging experience of my (already challenging!) life. You are always there for me, supporting and holding me, and your love is what makes everything I do possible. Linda – your WhatsApp memes and messages are *everything*. Thank you, and I love you.

To my children, Finlay and Amy, and stepchildren Tia and Sienna, thank you for your patience. I know I don't always get it right, but one day when you are grownups, you'll understand that my intentions were, and are, always done with all my love. I love you, and am proud of all of you, and can't wait to see what adventures await you.

To Lin, my "other mum" and right-hand woman. Thank you for just being there, especially when I needed it most and was too ashamed to ask for help. I love you.

To all my This Girl Is On Fire community and team – I know things didn't work out as we'd hoped, but I still think that we were part of something incredibly special. We did do some good in the world, even if it wasn't at the scale that I'd hoped for; every little helps, and I'm proud of the dent we made.

And finally, to my husband and wingman Nick. Thank you for letting me write all the ugly stuff as well as the good stuff; it takes a strong man to let his wife tell the world about the bits he doesn't get right, alongside the many things he does, and I love that you see the bigger picture in everything. What a ride we've had, and this is only our first decade! You are my "bestest good friend", my soulmate, and the love of my life, and if ever I was meant to go to hell and back, I'm glad that it was with you. Although I think I'm ready for some peace and quiet now – just putting it out there.

# Resources
# & Further Reading

## Chapter 1: Phew, It's Not Just Me

Burgo, Joseph, *Shame: Free Yourself, Find Joy And Build True Self-Esteem*, Watkins Publishing, 2018

## Chapter 2: Timing Is Everything

Augsburger, David W, *Pastoral Counseling Across Cultures*, Westminster John Knox Press, 1986

*Diary of a CEO* podcast by Steve Bartlett: candid interviews exploring entrepreneurship, personal growth, mental health, leadership, and life lessons. stevenbartlett.com/doac

## Chapter 3: "You CANNOT Work in Starbucks"

Financielle: the founders Laura Pomfret and her sister Holly Holland are wonderfully refreshing when it comes to talking about financial stuff. Their blog is brilliant, as is their podcast; I have recommended it to all the young women in our family to try and get them out of their Klarna habit, and to see that budgeting is cool. I wish I'd had them in my life years ago.
financielle.com

Money Supermarket: helpful, down-to-earth advice that doesn't make you feel stupid for needing to look it up. I subscribed to the newsletter, checked my credit score (yup, it was off-the-scale *bad*) and started making tiny changes to how I did my banking. I felt like I was at least taking back a tiny bit of control.
moneysupermarket.com

## Chapter 4: Behind the Scenes

Caroline Castrillon, "How To Survive A Toxic Manager In Any Workplace", *Forbes*
forbes.com/sites/carolinecastrillon/2025/03/05/how-to-recognize-and-survive-a-toxic-manager-in-any-workplace/?utm_
James Jenkins, "How to Survive and Thrive in A Toxic Workplace", Mental Health Wellness Online
mentalhealthwellnessmhw.com/blog/how-to-survive-and-thrive-in-a-toxic-workplace?utm
Anna Whitehouse: the journalist and campaigner for flexible working's website and Instagram offers news, stories, events, and reviews.
motherpukka.co.uk
Instagram @mother_pukka

## Chapter 5: Love Hurts, and Other Truths

Glover Tawab, Nedra, *Set Boundaries, Find Peace: A Guide to Reclaiming Yourself*, TarcherPerigee/HarperCollins, 2021
Domestic abuse support UK
Women's Aid: charity supporting women and children affected by domestic abuse, providing refuge, advocacy, and safety services.
womensaid.org.uk
Refuge: organisation providing emergency housing, practical help, and emotional support.
nationaldahelpline.org.uk
Domestic abuse support US
The National Domestic Violence Hotline: provides 24/7 confidential support, crisis intervention, safety planning, and referrals.
thehotline.org

Safe Horizon: support for survivors of domestic violence, offering
    shelter, counselling, and legal help.
safehorizon.org

## Chapter 6: Let's Talk About Sex, Baby

Nagoski, Emily, *Come As You Are: The Surprising New Science that Will
    Transform Your Sex Life*, Simon & Schuster, 2015
Camilla Graziani and Meredith L Chivers, "Sexual Shame and Women's
    Sexual Functioning", MDPI, 2024
mdpi.com/2411-5118/5/4/47?utm_
Stacey Diane A Litam and Megan Speciale, "Deconstructing Sexual
    Shame: Implications for Clinical Counselors and Counselor
    Educators", *Journal of Counseling Sexology & Sexual Wellness,*
    volume 3, issue 1, 2021
digitalcommons.unf.edu/cgi/viewcontent.
    cgi?article=1045&context=jcssw&utm_
The Children's Commissioner report on young people and pornography:
childrenscommissioner.gov.uk/
    resource/a-lot-of-it-is-actually-just-abuse-young-people-and-
    pornography/
Shan Boodram: certified sex educator, relationship expert, and podcaster.
@shanboodram
loversbyshan.com
Sex therapy advice and support UK
UK Council for Psychotherapy: find accredited therapists, understand
    psychotherapy, explore therapy types, and access guidance safely.
    psychotherapy.org.uk
Relate: relationship support, counselling, therapy, and education for
    couples, families, and individuals.
relate.org.uk/sex-counselling
LGBTQ+ therapy and support: find specialist gender, sex and
    relationship therapists.
pinktherapy.com
Sex therapy advice and support US
Psychology Today: find a therapist with a searchable directory of

licensed professionals, plus self-help resources. psychologytoday.
com/us/therapists?category=sex-therapy&utm_
Society for Sex Therapy & Research: sexual health information,
educational resources, and a directory of certified sex therapists.
sstarnet.org/find-therapist?utm

**Chapter 7: Is It Me, or Is It Hot in Here?**
Kaye, Dr Philippa, *The Science of the Menopause*, DK, 2024
McLean, Andrea, *Confessions of a Menopausal Woman,* Bantam Press,
2018
Taylor, Katie, *Midlife Matters*, DK Red, 2025
Professor Dame Lesley Regan, "Women's Health Strategy for England",
Department of Health & Social Care
gov.uk/government/publications/womens-health-strategy-for-england/
womens-health-strategy-for-england
British Menopause Society: practical advice on the menopause and
midlife health, including symptom guidance, treatment options, and
lifestyle tips.
thebms.org.uk
North American Menopause Society: menopause information, symptom
management tips, treatment guidance, lifestyle advice, and
resources.
menopause.org

**Chapter 8: Breaking the Chain of Generational Shame**
Maté, Gabor, *Scattered Minds: The Origins and Healing of Attention
Deficit Disorder*, Vermillion, 2019
Stephen Graham interview about *Adolescence*:
netflix.com/tudum/articles/adolescence-stephen-graham-interview

**Chapter 9: Nasty Gals**

Brown, Dr Brené, *Daring Greatly: How The Courage to be Vulnerable Transforms The Way We Live, Love, Parent and Lead*, Penguin Life, 2015

Aline Holzwarth, "The Three Laws Of Human Behaviour"
behavioraleconomics.com/the-three-laws-of-human-behavior/

"Why Do People Troll", BBC Bitesize
bbc.co.uk/bitesize/articles/zfmkrj6

"How Can I Stop Trolling People", GoodTherapy® blog
goodtherapy.org/blog/dear-gt/why-do-i-troll-people-on-the-internet-how-can-i-stop

Mind: information and support on mental health issues.
mind.org.uk/information-support

**Chapter 10: You're a Long Time Dead**

Diana Nyad interview with CNN
youtube.com/watch?v=plu-4wTZqf4

BBC documentary *The Great Gangster Film Fraud*
bbc.co.uk/programmes/p03fm01s/p03flsqr

# Notes

1   Salma Hayek, "Own Your Mistakes", Bystander Revolution, 1 October
    2014, available at: https://www.imdb.com/title/tt4078868/
2   John Bradshaw, "Bradshaw On The Family: A Revolutionary Way of
    Self-Discovery" (Florida, Health Communications, 1988), available at:
    https://archive.org/details/bradshawonthefam00brad
3   Erin Hanson, "What If I Fly", available at:
    https://www.goodreads.com/
    quotes/1236928-there-is-freedom-waiting-for-you-on-the-breezes-of
4   Michael Lewis, "The Self-Conscious Emotions" in Encyclopedia on
    Early Childhood Development online, September 2022, available at
    https://www.child-encyclopedia.com/emotions/according-experts/
    self-conscious-emotions
5   Lindsay Dodgson, "A psychotherapist says there are four stages of
    shame", *The Independent*, 4 April 2018, available at: https://www.
    independent.co.uk/life-style/health-and-families/healthy-living/
    different-types-of-shame-psychology-a8287981.html
6   Salma Hayek, "Own Your Mistakes", Bystander Revolution, 2014,
    available at: https://www.youtube.com/watch?v=r1CCrKJF3NQ

7   Tom Ford, "From Fashion to Film", interview with Terry Gross, *Fresh Air* (NPR), 14 Dec 2009, available at: https://freshairarchive.org/segments/tom-ford-fashion-film-single-man

8   Daniel McCarthy et al, "Evaluating the Impact of Privacy Regulation on E-Commerce Firms: Evidence from Apple's App Tracking Transparency", October 2024, available at: https://www.rhsmith.umd.edu/research/small-businesses-take-big-hit-apples-privacy-regulation

9   Toby Murray and Nikki Bond, "Debts and Despair", The Money and Metal Health Policy Institute, available at: https://www.moneyandmentalhealth.org/publications/debts-and-despair/

10  Theodore Roosevelt, "Citizenship in a Republic", read at the Sorbonne, Paris, 23 April 1910, available at: bit.ly/483kr7r

11  Employment in the UK statistical bulletin, Office for National Statistics (ONS), 13 August 2024, available at: https://www.ons.gov.uk/employmentandlabourmarket/peopleinwork/employmentandemployeetypes/bulletins/employmentintheuk/august2024

12  Age UK policy position paper on employment, December 2022, available at: https://www.ageuk.org.uk/siteassets/documents/policy-positions/active-communities/employment-policy-position---december-2022.pdf

13  "Work, the State of Ageing" 2023–24, Centre for Ageing Better, available at: https://ageing-better.org.uk/work-state-ageing-2023-4

14  Charles Horton Cooley, *Human Nature and the Societal Order* (New York: Charles Scribner's Sons, 1902), available at: https://www.gutenberg.org/ebooks/75145

15  Anna J Dreyer, Dale Stephen, Robyn Human, et al, "Risky Decision Making Under Stressful Conditions: Men and Women With Smaller Cortisol Elevations Make Riskier Social and Economic Decisions", *Frontiers in Psychology*, 04 February 2022, available at: https://www.frontiersin.org/journals/psychology/articles/10.3389/fpsyg.2022.810031/full#B50

16  Sarah Foster, "Women are more likely to feel stressed about their finances than men – here's what to do about it", Bankrate.net, 1 June 2022, available at: https://www.bankrate.com/banking/federal-reserve/why-women-feel-more-financial-stress/

17  Dr Chris Dawson, "Gender differences in optimism, loss aversion and attitudes towards risk", *British Journal of Psychology*, 9 June 2023, available at: https://bpspsychub.onlinelibrary.wiley.com/doi/full/10.1111/bjop.12668

18  Wan-chin Kuo, Linda D Oakley, Roger L Brown et al, "Gender Differences in the Relationship Between Financial Stress and Metabolic Abnormalities", National Library of Medicine, 1 January 2022, available at: https://pmc.ncbi.nlm.nih.gov/articles/PMC8106736/

19  "Pregnancy and Maternity-Related Discrimination and Disadvantage", Equality and Human Rights Commission, available at: https://www.equalityhumanrights.com/sites/default/files/mothers_report_-_bis-16-146-pregnancy-and-maternity-related-discrimination-and-disadvantage-experiences-of-mothers_1.pdf

20  Employment Relations (Flexible Working) Act 2023, available at: https://www.legislation.gov.uk/ukpga/2023/33/notes/division/10/index.htm?utm

21  Dita Von Teese quote, available at: https://tim.blog/2019/07/31/the-tim-ferriss-show-transcripts-dita-von-teese-the-queen-of-burlesque-379/?utm_

22  Nedra Glover Tawab, *Set Boundaries, Find Peace: A Guide to Reclaiming Yourself*, (New York, TarcherPerigee/HarperCollins, 2021) page XVII

23  Jennifer Aniston, "For the Record", open letter to the Huff Post, July 2016, available at: https://www.huffpost.com/entry/for-the-record_b_57855586e4b03fc3ee4e626f

24  Gaby Hinsliff, "Taylor Swift: engaged, mummy-tracked and doomed to tradwifedom? You really haven't been listening", The Guardian, 28 August 2025, available at: https://www.theguardian.com/

commentisfree/2025/aug/28/
taylor-swift-engaged-married-women-music?utm_source

25  Belinda Luscombe, "What Gisèle Pelicot's Case Can—and
Can't—Change for Survivors", *Time magazine*, 19 December 2024,
available at: https://time.com/7203435/
what-gisele-pelicots-case-cant-change/

26  Alfred, Lord Tennyson, "In Memoriam A.H.H." (1850), Project
Gutenberg

27  *Love Actually* opening scene, screenplay by Richard Curtis, Universal
Pictures, 2003, available at:
https://www.youtube.com/watch?v=HcKjdBB6SUk

28  Emily Nagoski, *Come As You Are: The Surprising New Science that Will
Transform Your Sex Life*, (London, Simon & Schuster, 2015) p.265

29  The Children's Commissioner report on young people and
pornography, 31 January 2023, available at:
https://www.childrenscommissioner.gov.uk/
resource/a-lot-of-it-is-actually-just-abuse-young-people-and-
pornography/

30  Camilla Graziani and Meredith L Chivers, "Sexual Shame and Women's
Sexual Functioning", 3 December 2024, MDPI, available at:
https://www.mdpi.com/2411-5118/5/4/47?utm_

31  Ibid

32  Medichecks Research on Attitudes to Women Seeking Medical
Support, available at:
https://www.medichecks.com/blogs/womens-health/
felt-dismissed-or-struggling-for-health-answers-read-this

33  "RCOG calls on new government to take urgent action on
gynaecology care crisis", RCOG, available at:
https://www.rcog.org.uk/news/
rcog-calls-on-new-government-to-take-urgent-action-on-gynaecology-
care-crisis/

34  Nitya Dintakurti, Shreya Kalyanasundaram, Prashant Jha, et al, "An
online survey and interview of GPs in the UK for assessing their
satisfaction regarding the medical training curriculum and NICE

guidelines for the management of menopause." *Post reproductive health* vol. 28,3 (2022), pp.137–141, available at: http://pubmed.ncbi. nlm.nih.gov/35639933/

35  "Menopause in the Workplace", The Fawcett Society 2022, available at: https://www.fawcettsociety.org.uk/Handlers/Download. ashx?IDMF=9672cf45-5f13-4b69-8882-1e5e643ac8a6

36  "Employment and Self-Employment by Sex and Age Group, UK, 2011–2022", Office of National Statistics, 3 May 2023, available at: https://www.ons.gov.uk/employmentandlabourmarket/peopleinwork/ employmentandemployeetypes/adhocs/ 1098employmentandselfemploymentbysexandagegroupuk2011to2022

37  Menopause Support and Services Bill, available at: https://bills. parliament.uk/bills/2897

38  NHS Menopause Update, Department of Health and Social Care, 23 October 2025, available at: https://www.gov.uk/government/news/ major-nhs-update-brings-menopause-into-routine-health-checks

39  "Government appoints first Menopause Employment Champion to improve workplace support", Department of Work And Pensions, 6 March 2023, available at: https://www.gov.uk/government/news/ government-appoints-first-menopause-employment-champion-to- improve workplace-support

40  "An Important Victory: Menopause will now be taught in UK secondary schools", Menopause Support, 4 July 2019, available at: https://bit.ly/44f8Fpr

41  Philip Baum's LinkedIn post https://www.linkedin.com/posts/ philip-baum-7400b38_menopause-activity-7313858151068434432-0OeR

42  Philip Larkin, "This Be The Verse", *The Complete Poems* (Faber & Faber, 2012), courtesy of Faber and Faber Ltd

43  Gabor Maté, "No two children have the same parents", Child Health BC, available at: https://www.youtube.com/watch?v=jbXqSEkwOPo

44  Gabor Maté on "Young Again with Kirsty Young", BBC Radio 4, 15 October 2024, available at:

https://www.bbc.co.uk/sounds/play/m0023ycy

45  Kristen Iverson interview with Stephen Graham, Netflix, 24 March 2025, available at: https://www.netflix.com/tudum/articles/adolescence-stephen-graham-interview

46  Alexander Pope, An Essay on Criticism, 1711

47  Brené Brown, *Daring Greatly* (Wyoming, Gotham Books, 2012) p.82

48  Anaïs Nin, *Seduction of the Minotaur* (1961), quote available at: https://www.theguardian.com/culture/2015/apr/07/anais-nin-author-social-media

49  Thomas J Scheff, "Shame and the Social Bond: A Sociological Theory", *Sociological Theory* (2000), available at: https://www.jstor.org/stable/223283?utm_source

50  Anna Peel, "In Caroline Flack: Search for the Truth, a Grieving Mother Tries to Clear Her Daughter's Name", *Vanity Fair,* 10 November 2025, available at:
https://www.vanityfair.com/hollywood/story/caroline-flack-docuseries-love-island?utm_

51  Archie Bland, "Media Fail to learn from Caroline Flack's death, her mother warns", *The Guardian,* 12 March 2021, available at: https://www.theguardian.com/tv-and-radio/2021/mar/12/caroline-flack-film-explores-medias-role-in-tv-stars-death?utm_

52  Saul McLeod, "Stanley Milgram Shock Experiment", *Simply Psychology,* 14 March 2025, available at: https://www.simplypsychology.org/milgram.html

53  Megan Grisham, "Ella Langley Says She's 'Grateful' After Taking Time Off For Health Struggles", *Country Rebel,* 11 September 2025, available at: https://countryrebel.com/ella-langley-says-shes-grateful-after-taking-time-off-for-health-struggles/

54  Sanjay Gupta interview with Diana Nyad on CNN, 3 September 2013, available at:
https://www.youtube.com/watch?v=plu-4wTZqf4

55  Diana Nyad, Never Ever Give Up, TEDWomen 2013, available at: https://www.ted.com/talks/diana_nyad_never_ever_give_up

56 Chris Greenwood, "Five 'Hollywood' fraudsters who conned Loose Women host Andrea McLean", *Daily Mail*, 25 March 2013, available at: https://www.dailymail.co.uk/news/article-2298937/A-Landscape-Of-Lies-Fraudsters-conned-Loose-Women-host-Andrea-McLean-3million-tax-scam-jailed.html

57 "The Great Gangster Film Fraud", BBC 4 Storyville, 2016, available at: https://www.bbc.co.uk/programmes/p03fm01s/p03flsqr

58 St John of the Cross, "Dark Night of the Soul", available at: https://en.wikipedia.org/wiki/Dark_Night_of_the_Soul

59 Martin Luther King Jr, *Strength to Love* (New York: Harper & Row, 1963), p.116

# About the Author

**Andrea McLean** is a *Sunday Times* bestselling author and speaker. She was formerly the longest-serving host of ITV's popular and multi-award winning daytime chat show *Loose Women*. A beloved figure in British television, Andrea brought her warmth and humour to the screen every lunchtime throughout her 24-year TV career, interviewing icons such as Oprah Winfrey, Beyoncé and Michael Bublé. Andrea has since relocated to Spain with her husband and their dog, Teddy, where she continues to write.